Bakers' secrets for making
amazing long-rise loaves at home

Slow Dough
REAL BREAD

CHRIS YOUNG
AND THE BAKERS OF THE REAL BREAD CAMPAIGN

NOURISH
EAT WELL, LIVE WELL

For Marika

Slow Dough: Real Bread
Chris Young

First published in the UK and USA in 2016 by
Nourish, an imprint of Watkins Media Limited
19 Cecil Court
London WC2N 4EZ

enquiries@nourishbooks.com

Managing Editor: Rebecca Woods
Editor: David Whitehouse
Design: Viki Ottewill
Production: Uzma Taj
Commissioned Photography: Victoria Harley
Food Stylist: Rebecca Woods
Prop Stylist: Linda Berlin

A CIP record for this book is available from the
British Library

ISBN: 978-1-84899-737-0

10 9 8 7 6 5 4 3 2 1

Typeset in Brandon Grotesque and Adobe Jenson Pro

Colour reproduction by XY Digital
Printed in China

Publisher's note:
While every care has been taken in compiling the recipes for
this book, Watkins Media Limited, or any other persons who
have been involved in working on this publication, cannot
accept responsibility for any errors or omissions, inadvertent
or not, that may be found in the recipes or text, nor for
any problems that may arise as a result of preparing one of
these recipes. If you are pregnant or breastfeeding or have
any special dietary requirements or medical conditions, it is
advisable to consult a medical professional before following
any of the recipes contained in this book.

Notes:
Unless otherwise stated:
• Use medium fruit and vegetables
• Use fresh ingredients, including herbs and spices
• Do not mix imperial and metric measurements
• 1 teaspoon = 5ml
  1 tablespoon = 15ml
  1 cup = 240ml

nourishbooks.com

Contents

Foreword

"You must be mad!" Derisive remarks such as this were once familiar to anyone announcing their intention to quit their job and start a microbakery, or even simply to make their own bread. After all, supermarket loaves are cheap as chips and they stay soft forever. Making your own is a waste of time and you'd have to be a crank to want to bake for a living.

Accusations of commercial naivety bordering on irrationality certainly came my way in the 1970s when I was starting a bakery in a small Cumbrian village using wholemeal/wholewheat flour from the local watermill. But 40 years on, sales of white loaves in the UK are down by 75% since 1974, with a concurrent rise in "brown" and wholemeal. Government figures don't reveal how much of the switch has been away from industrial loaves in favour of Real Bread, but they confirm that the bread scene in Britain is changing like never before.

It was E.F. Schumacher (author of *Small is Beautiful*) who observed that a crank is "a small lever that causes revolutions". Perhaps it's the sense of an uncontrollable reordering of familiar ways that so perturbs the multi-billion-pound loaf industry, whose market is in evident disarray. But to ordinary citizens, this is a benign ferment (of micro-organisms) whose product will be bread that's better for individuals, communities and the biosphere.

If that sounds a rather grandiose claim, this book justifies it by setting out the differences between Real Bread and industrial loaves in an admirably accessible way. The message boils down to "out with additives, in with fermentation time" and here simplicity and practicality are leavened with the wry humour (not to mention plentiful puns) essential to the communication of important truths.

As Chris points out in his introduction to this book, one of the Real Bread Campaign's main tasks is to defend the integrity of concepts such as "sourdough". "artisan" and "craft" against the opportunism of food companies that mislead the public by applying these words to industrial products and processes that are far from the "real thing".

This matters, because reducing the mounting burden of diet-related ill health in the UK will only happen if citizens can make well-informed decisions about what to eat. Choosing good bread isn't that easy, partly because its real goodness is not always evident on the surface, and partly because Real Bread involves much more than well-made dough. The dominant model of loaf production and distribution looks precarious: its high-energy, long-distance, globalized business model isn't relevant to the de-carbonized economy that the future requires. A dysfunctional commoditized grain system ensures

that the flour for our bread is poorer in nutrients than it once was, even as the enormous cost of heart disease, obesity and diabetes indicates that we should be eating less, but better. Cheap loaves with little in them have had their day. What we do need are more real bakers whose growing skills are rewarded with fair pay, self-respect and a sense of fulfilment.

One of the most nonsensical accusations made against the Campaign by its detractors has been that, by drawing attention to the way industrial loaves are made and the undeclared ingredients used in their production, we are somehow "dragging the whole baking industry down". But rather than collude in the ridiculous pretence that all loaves are equally good, the Campaign encourages professional bakers and amateurs alike to make the best bread they can, using flour from nutritious grains, fermented slowly for maximum digestibility and nourishment, and enjoyed as close to their place of origin as possible. This is where information and a sense of connection transform bread's meaning and the power contained within it. The home-baked loaf that you place on the family table, made from a named flour, perhaps even grown by a known farmer, isn't savoured by those who eat it because it's cheap, but because it is immeasurably rich with the associations that make

life worth living. The same applies to Real Bread made nearby by people whom you know or can get to know.

Successful revolutions involve a change of power. The Real Bread revolution is about more even than imaginative career changes, artisan bakery start-ups or niche markets. It's about peacefully and productively taking the power to make bread back into our own hands. This book shows why and how. If everyone who reads it both uses it and joins the movement, we'll get closer to our goal of communities in which everyone lives within walking distance of Real Bread. Roll on, as they say.

Andrew Whitley
CO-FOUNDER OF THE REAL BREAD CAMPAIGN

The Fight for Better Bread

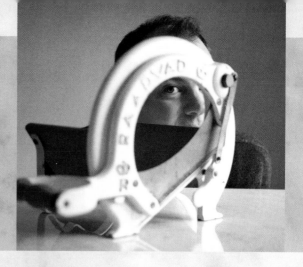

In the words of my father-in-law and dad, respectively: slow down and get real!

Since March 2009, I have been the coordinator of the Real Bread Campaign, part of the food and farming charity Sustain. Through my work, I've come into contact with some great people, many of whom also happen to be brilliant bakers but whose work goes unsung. Believing their praises do deserve to be sung, I put out an open call through our international supporters' network for long-rise recipes to form the basis of a book celebrating Real Bread and the people who make it. This is that book.

So, why have we produced a book of breads that take longer to make? Some of the artificial additives industrial loaf fabricators throw into their doughs are used in their drive to reduce one very important natural ingredient: time. Even some domestic recipe writers seem to be in a race to the finish line, instructing their readers to use fast-action yeast, added sugar and warm proving, declaring with glee how little time the loaf will take.

Increasingly, however, Real Bread bakers are reminding people that long and slow tends to be far more satisfying than a quick finish. Far from farinaceous folly, a long-proved dough has more time to develop flavour, tends to produce a less crumbly loaf and, in the case of genuine sourdough, might even offer health benefits.

I'm not a professional baker, which is part of the message of this doughy tome: You might not be an artisan baker (yet) but you can still make brilliant Real Bread. While the bakers from whom we harvested these recipes are experts, you don't have to be one to bake their loaves. The people we most had in mind when cooking up this book are those passionate home bakers, who've got the hang of basic loaves and now want to further their flour arranging. We hope that some professionals will enjoy it, too, and we encourage all of you to experiment with the recipes to make them work for you, make them your own and make the best Real Bread you can.

Chris Young

NB: In compiling this book, I have rewritten and often tweaked recipes that were donated to us for this book. In some cases, the changes have been significant and what appears on the page might better be described as "inspired by", rather than created by a particular baker, but as I didn't want to take credit away from any of them, their names still appear. I'm sure you'll love the loaves but if you're not utterly pleased as punch with one, please don't blame the named baker.

If you donated a recipe and the way we made a loaf is different from the way you do, or yours was one of many we simply couldn't cram in – sorry!

WHERE WE STAND

As I live and work in London, I know more about the bread of Britain than of other countries. Until relatively recently, the future of bread in Britain looked bleak. Following the Second World War, the number of independent bakeries headed into what seemed a permanent decline, with a handful of industrial giants and multiple retailers rising to dominance and helping to speed their demise.

A particularly dark day for Real Bread historians came in July 1961, when the British Baking Industries Research Association unleashed what later became known as the Chorleywood Bread Process (CBP), which takes a shortcut through dough's natural fermentation and "ripening" time, slashing it from hours or even days to minutes.

Convinced by costly marketing campaigns to believe that one CBP loaf was as good as any other, we began to look to our supermarkets for sandwich rolls, using the same squeeze test we might use for toilet rolls. As a nation, we conspired in a race to the bottom, and by the end of the 1990s we were challenging anyone who had the temerity to charge more than about 7p a loaf. Nope, that's not a typo: in 1999 at least one supermarket dropped the price of its "value" range own-brand loaves far below even the cost of production, to just *seven pence*.

Chemistry set

To meet their need for speed, Big Bakers lace their dough with so-called "processing aids" and other artificial additives, which help the dough conform to the stresses of the process; to become stretchy enough to rise high and quickly, and then to have strength enough to stay risen during baking. Other substances might be used to deter the growth of mould and to help the finished loaf to stay softer for longer.

A few thousand years of people eating Real Bread has proved beyond any doubt that it is safe – no, actually *good* for the vast majority of us. Compared to this, artificial additives have only been subjected to a relatively short period of testing before being declared safe (or "generally recognized as safe" as the more pragmatic US Food and Drink Administration put it) for food manufacturers using them in their products.

No one knows for sure, however, if there might be any adverse effects from long-term consumption of the artificial additives found in the modern industrial loaf and across many people's diets in other heavily processed foods. Can we trust that these things, either individually or in the endless combinations they'll turn up in a supermarket shopping basket, are truly safe? History is littered with a veritable chemistry set of substances once used by industrial millers and bakers, only to be withdrawn or banned. They include azodicarbonamide (banned in countries including the UK and Australia but legal in others, including the USA), benzoyl peroxide, agene (nitrogen trichloride, banned in the 1940s) and potassium bromate.

Clean loaf or just clean label?

Though some of the differences between Real Bread and industrial loaves may be obvious, labelling and marketing regulations, and the way they are policed, can leave loopholes that deny shoppers the right to know exactly what they're getting.

Knowing that many of us find a litany of E numbers off-putting, some manufacturers are now turning to so-called processing aids. By a quirk of EU law, if an industrial loaf (or other food) manufacturer deems an artificial additive to be a "processing aid", it does not have to appear on the label, as long as any "residues do not present any health risk and do not have any technological effect on the finished product". As a consequence, suppliers often market these additives as "clean label" or "label friendly". Companies may defend the use of processing aids with comments along the lines of "we always comply with the law", which is nice to know. Another defence is that "they get used up during manufacture", despite the fact that their use may, quite legally, "result in the unintentional but technically unavoidable presence of residues of the substance or its derivatives in the final product".

The Great British Fake Off

Like the word "bread" itself, the terms "artisan" and "craft" have no legal definition. Anyone can call themselves an artisan or craft baker and market their loaves as such. The production methods used may not be obvious and, in the case of loaves that aren't pre-packed – such as those from a supermarket in-store "bakery" – you'll struggle to find whether or not artificial additives have been used.

An allegedly "freshly baked" unwrapped loaf sold by a retailer may have been manufactured a long time ago in a factory far away, then chilled or frozen. Having then been re-baked in a retailer's "loaf tanning salon" increases the energy consumed in production, and results in a loaf that may well stale faster than a genuinely fresh one. Not that you'd know any of that, so you could be forgiven for making a like-for-like comparison with a loaf of Real Bread from an independent bakery, which helps to sustain more skilled jobs per loaf for local people making genuinely freshly baked bread without the use of artificial additives. Which part of this is fair on you the shopper or a genuine artisan baker?

But while the wrapped, sliced industrial loaf still accounts for the largest percentage of the "bread" market in Britain, it is in decline, with sales falling more than £100 million a year. Retail industry research over the past few years has been consistent in reporting "artisan" and "speciality" bread as being the only sectors of the market seeing significant growth in sales.

THE REAL BREAD CAMPAIGN

From Roman and medieval statutes, through 19th-century wholemeal advocates, including Sylvester

Graham and Thomas Allinson, and national newspaper campaigns in the early 20th century, and the Campaign for Real Bread that ran in Britain as the 1970s turned into the 1980s, the fight for better bread is perhaps as old as bread itself.

Since the 1990s, the number of bakers working tirelessly to share their passion for (and loaves of) Real Bread has grown enormously, as has the interest for what they make and how they make it. A milestone in the origins of the current Real Bread Campaign, which works to unite these people as a coordinated movement, was the 2006 publication of Andrew Whitley's book *Bread Matters*. An attempt at putting down the knowledge he'd built up founding and running The Village Bakery Melmerby, between 1976 and 2002, *Bread Matters* sets out what has gone wrong and, importantly, what we can all do to help change things for the better.

Immediately upon the book's publication, people took it as a manifesto and began asking Andrew how they could join his fight that so well reflected and represented their own beliefs, personal experience of finding industrial loaves hard to stomach or, in the cases of many bakers, their ways of bread making. After a year or two of this, he turned to his friends at Sustain and asked if the charity fancied being the organization that would join the dots, bringing together everyone who cares about the issues.

In 2008, Sustain set up the Real Bread Campaign website to lay out its beliefs, aims and plans, as well as a Real Bread Finder map to help people track down additive-free loaves locally. Quickly, this attracted the interest of hundreds of people, and after a series of open meetings, Andrew and Sustain officially launched the Campaign on 26 November of that year. Since then it has attracted thousands of supporters in more than 20 countries. Behind a rallying cry of "not all loaves are created equal!", together we've been finding and sharing ways to make bread better for us, better for our communities and better for the planet.

GET REAL

Everyone will have his or her own idea of what Real Bread is, so for the record, here's how the Campaign defines it:

Real Bread is made without the use of processing aids or any other artificial additives.

Simple, eh? Technically, the only ingredients essential for making bread are flour and water. With these two things you can make unleavened flatbreads, or nurture the yeasts and bacteria naturally present in the flour to create a sourdough culture for leavening. Anything else is, by definition, unnecessary. That said, without a little salt, bread can taste bland and you might prefer to let someone else culture the yeast, rather than do it yourself. We also celebrate the use of other, natural ingredients.

Community

The Real Bread Campaign doesn't wish to deny any industrial baker their job, but believes that a small, independent Real Bread bakery is of greater benefit to both its bakers and to other people in its local community. These benefits might include:

+ Skilled, meaningful jobs for local people producing food for their neighbours.

+ More jobs-per-loaf than an industrial loaf factory.

+ Opportunities for social interaction between employees and customers.

+ Support for the local high street and economy: money spent with a local business is more likely to be reinvested locally.

+ Potential to support local producers, growers or other smaller or more ethical suppliers, by providing an outlet for their goods.

+ The chance to shop on foot, by bike or public transport, rather than having to drive to an out-of-town megamarket.

Honesty

To protect shoppers and independent businesses alike, the Real Bread Campaign calls for an Honest Crust Act in the UK that will require:

+ All bakers and retailers to provide full lists of ingredients (and any "processing aids" or other artificial additives used) on all loaf bags. In the case of unwrapped loaves, this information must be displayed clearly at the point of sale.

+ Meaningful, legal and enforced definitions for the terms "fresh" and "freshly baked" when used in the marketing of loaves – not to be used for "bake-off" products.

+ Meaningful, legal definitions for "sourdough", "artisan", "wholegrain" and "craft".

+ Section six of the Bread and Flour Regulations 1998 to be tightened and fully enforced to ensure the likes of dried gluten and soya flour do not make their way into loaves sold as wholemeal.

In the meantime, the Campaign calls upon all bakers and retailers voluntarily to provide full information about their loaves, stop marketing bake-off loaves as fresh, and ensure that the terms "sourdough", "artisan" and "craft" are used appropriately.

The Real Bread Campaign kneads YOU!

Whether you're a domestic or professional Real Bread baker (or simply love eating their loaves and just bought this book because you like the pictures) we'd love you to join our mutually supportive, international community and help support our charity's work.

Read more and join the Real Bread Campaign today at **realbreadcampaign.org**.

Real Slow Bread

Some domestic baking recipe writers and teachers suggest that dough must be kept somewhere warm to rise, or that yeast left anywhere cooler than their fevered brows will DIE! What they overlook is the fact that fresh yeast is generally stored in the refrigerator (at a far-from-balmy 1–3°C/34–37°F) and that a standard piece of professional bakery kit is a retarder, which is basically a big dough fridge.

Another product of their need for speed is the relatively high level of yeast you find in some recipes: the more of these microscopic, gas-burping dough monsters (which, if you have kids, is a great way to introduce bread science to *your* little monsters) you throw into the mix, the less time it will take them to generate the necessary amount of carbon dioxide.

A third trick up the speed freak's sleeve is the addition of sugar, be that refined or in another form, such as honey or agave syrup. This puts the yeast on a "high", and into a CO_2-producing overdrive. There is, however, more than enough energy contained in the flour, which the yeast is eminently capable of obtaining for itself. In fact, beyond a certain level of added sugar, the yeast struggles to cope.

And that's all before a baker reaches for the crutch of the aforementioned artificial additive arsenal . . .

So, what's wrong with speeding things up? Why would you want to delay the opportunity to tear into a freshly baked loaf of Real Bread, slather it with butter and tuck in? Why does any of this matter?

AGED TO PERFECTION

For many people, allowing their dough time to "do what a dough's gotta do" is simply a matter of good taste. Yes, you can bang out a loaf using warm water and a sachet of instant yeast in an hour or so, but you might be short changing yourself. Real Bread is a natural product and, just as with a whole range of food and drink, from ripening fruit to maturing beef, whisky, wine or cheese, time is essential in getting the very best product.

During this time, all sorts of biochemical alchemy goes on that, ultimately, will result in a texture, depth and complexity of flavour and aroma that can't be rushed or synthesized, whatever the pedlars of "bread flavour" (I kid you not) to big industry or "artisan sourdough" packet mixes to unsuspecting home bakers might say. You might also find that a long fermented loaf is less crumbly and stales more slowly.

Time is on your side

Happily, this extra time need not eat into *your* time: it can in fact buy you time while the dough gets on with it. Perhaps counterintuitively, using a recipe with less yeast and letting dough rise slowly somewhere cooler, in some cases all day or even overnight, allows you to go off and do something else.

You may think that great flavour and a relaxed baking schedule are reasons enough to slow things down, but when it comes to sourdough, there might be more . . .

SOUR POWER

Right, stop chewing at the back, it's time for a science lesson . . .

Sourdough is leavened using a culture of yeasts and lactic acid bacteria (LAB) that occur naturally all around us, particularly on the surface of cereal grains. Occurring in lower concentrations, and not the results of a century and a half of baker's yeast breeding programmes, these "wild" yeasts take longer to get their mojo working. During the hours that dough leavened in this way needs to rise, all sorts of weird and wonderful things go on, some of which might be beneficial health-wise, including:

+ A change in the parts of gluten responsible for triggering the coeliac response and non-coeliac gluten sensitivity

+ A reduction of phytic acid, an "anti-nutrient" found in bran that binds with certain nutrients, including calcium, magnesium, zinc and iron, meaning that the body can't make use of them

+ An increase in levels of available B vitamins

+ LAB can bring about changes during fermentation that lower the glycaemic index (GI) of bread, which can be handy for people challenged by diabetes and obesity

One of the motivations behind the Real Bread Campaign's creation was people saying that they found industrial loaves hard to digest but that they could enjoy genuine sourdough, and in some cases a wider range of long-fermented Real Breads. But why might that be the case? Despite a few compelling studies and a chorus of voices, there has been far too little research to say any of these things for sure. The Campaign continues to call for adequate investment into research that could lead to these and other potential benefits either being proved beyond reasonable doubt, or ruled out.

. . . and when you find out that LAB are essential to preserved foods such as cheese and kimchi, it should come as no surprise to learn that genuine sourdough loaves tend to last longer than commercially yeasted ones . . . well, if you don't eat them first.

TYPES OF REAL BREAD

All bread in the world can be divided into just a handful of types according to how they are made. As this book is all about long, slow fermentation, we have split them into chapters according to how they are leavened:

+ **Pre-ferment** – dough made in two stages using a pre-ferment often based on baker's yeast, some with more yeast added later as well

+ **Long ferment** – dough made in a single-stage process with baker's yeast

+ **Sourdough** – dough leavened only using a sourdough starter

You will also find enriched and laminated doughs dotted around within these chapters, so the definitions of these have been included, too.

Pre-ferment

A pre-ferment comprises flour, water and yeast, which is left to ferment before adding the bulk of the flour and other ingredients used in a dough. The yeast used to make a pre-ferment can be commercial (baker's) or, while we have separated sourdough loaves into their own chapter in this book, in the form of a sourdough starter.

A pre-ferment can range in hydration from a loose batter to a stiff dough. It might also contain salt and, in the case of old dough, perhaps fat and other ingredients. There are several reasons a baker might want – or need – to use a pre-ferment:

Yeast Vigour

An analogy for getting the fermentation underway might be giving the yeast a good run-up. In a straight dough it has to go from nought to full throttle

TYPES OF PRE-FERMENT

- **Batter pre-ferment** (e.g. poolish) A mixture that has a high water content, perhaps 100% hydration – i.e. equal weights of flour and water. Typically made with a tiny percentage of baker's yeast.

- **Dough pre-ferment** (e.g. biga) A stiffer dough of perhaps 50–60% hydration – i.e. water weight is 50–60% that of the flour. Typically made with a tiny percentage of baker's yeast.

- **Old dough** (e.g. *pâte fermentée*) A piece of unbaked dough kept back from a previous bake, or made especially, that is fully proved and then added to a new dough.

- **Sourdough culture** (e.g. *desem*, *sauerteig*, *lievito madre*, mother, chef, starter etc.) Water is added to flour to culture the yeasts it contains until they are capable of raising dough.

straight away. Working up a full head of steam (how many metaphors can I mix in here?) is particularly useful when making an enriched dough, where the high levels of sugar will hinder the yeast.

Gluten Strength

During the fermentation of a stiffer pre-ferment (like a traditional biga) and especially in a sourdough, acid levels will increase. This assists gluten formation, and so is useful when working with weaker flours.

Dough Extensibility

Conversely, in a more liquid starter, particularly one fermented at room temperature without salt, protease (an enzyme that breaks down protein) activity will be increased. This will make the dough more extensible or stretchy.

Bread Flavour

During fermentation, all sorts of dough alchemy goes on, which helps create flavour and aroma compounds. As time increases, so do the amounts of these, so it is a useful addition to a shorter process recipe as a way of improving texture and flavour.

If you want to get serious with pre-ferments, do some research online or in baking manuals to find out about the effects that time, temperature, yeast quantities and so on will have on them, and on your Real Bread. You'll also get to read endless disagreements over the true definitions of biga, sponge, poolish etc.

Straight process plain dough (long ferment)

This is any recipe in which all the flour, baker's yeast, water and salt (plus any other ingredients) are mixed and fermented together in one go. For the purposes of this book, all the straight process doughs are left to ferment for longer periods.

Sourdough

Sourdough is the oldest method of making leavened bread. Historians generally seem to agree the first leavened loaf probably came out of an oven in Egypt, sometime between 6,000 and 3,500 years ago. Genuine sourdough bread is leavened (i.e. made to rise – like lever, it comes from a Latin word meaning "to raise") using only a culture of yeasts and (probiotic) "friendly" lactic acid bacteria, which live happy lives on the surface of cereal grains.

Culture Club

Yeasts and bacteria live in and all around us, including on the outside of wheat and other cereals. Milling mixes these microbes into the resulting flour, so if you take some (particularly wholemeal) and provide a suitable (basically warm and wet) environment, the microorganisms will thrive. Eventually there will be enough yeast cells burping carbon dioxide as a by-product of their respiration to make bread rise. At the same time, the throng of bacteria will increase. This is sourdough culture or leaven.

The interaction of these bacteria and the products of their respiration (including lactic and acetic acids) contribute to the flavour, texture and aroma of the bread. Additional benefits in a genuine sourdough include slowing the staling of the loaf.

Not Yeast Free

It is a myth (and ignorant, or perhaps even misleading, marketing) to say that sourdough bread is made without yeast. All sourdough cultures contain one or more species of yeast. In some cases these yeasts might even include the same species (*Saccharomyces cerevisiae*) that is sold as baker's and brewer's yeast. It is unlikely, however, that even if *S. cerevisiae* is present in a sourdough culture that it will be genetically identical to a commercial strain.

Specific strains of *S. cerevisiae* have been chosen over years of selective breeding, for example for their ability to produce large volumes of carbon dioxide, and to generate different flavour profiles in the finished product. A strain of genetically modified baker's yeast was approved for use in the UK some years ago, but it has not and is not being used in bread making. Some brands, however, might not be able to be labelled as GM free, if the growth medium (e.g. soya molasses) used was from a GM plant.

One further thought – yeasts die at around 60°C/140°F. As the internal temperature of bread should reach at least 95°C/205°F during baking, by the time a properly made loaf of any type of bread is ready to eat, it will contain no live yeast, only dead cells and by-products.

As for whether or not someone who has a yeast allergy or intolerance can eat sourdough bread, personal experience may produce the only reliable answer, but our advice would be to get tested by an expert in food allergies and intolerances.

Control

As well as one or more types of yeast, sourdough cultures contain lactobacilli (lactic acid bacteria) that produce both lactic and acetic acids. A key part of mastering sourdough is keeping the concentration and ratio of these acids in balance. Too much acetic acid and the bread will taste very sharp and perhaps vinegary (it is the same acid that is found in vinegar), whereas bread with too little acetic acid and a higher level of lactic acid might not have any discernible sourdough characteristics.

Liquid Sourdough Starter

Now, unless you bought this book for its ornamental value or to prop up a wobbly table, something you'll be using a lot of is a sourdough starter.

The recipe (if you can call two ingredients that) on the following page is both simple and effective. Rye grains seem to host very large microbe populations and as they live on the outside of the grain, your chances improve when using wholemeal flour, and it makes sense to use organic flour as the crop won't have been sprayed with fungicides.

A plastic container with a lid is convenient for storage because if your starter gets frisky, the lid will simply pop off, whereas a glass jar with a screwtop or metal clip seal could crack or shatter.

The amount of flour you use isn't important so we've started small, as instructions that tell you to throw portions of your starter away just seem wasteful. Please keep to the 1:1 ratio, though.

To Convert Your Starter to Wheat

Although you can use the rye starter for wheat breads, you might prefer to convert it by replacing the rye flour in refreshments with wheat flour (white or wholemeal/wholewheat) until it is all wheat. Alternatively, you can use wheat flour from the word go: again, wholemeal/wholewheat will give you a better chance of success. Whether you keep separate rye, white wheat, wholemeal/wholegrain wheat, and even other starters on the go, or just one, is up to you.

SOURDOUGH STARTER

Daily: days one to five (ish)

30g/1oz/3½ tbsp rye flour
30g/1oz/2 tbsp water (at about 20°C/68°F)

On each of the first five days, put equal amounts of flour and water into your container, mix, close and leave at room temperature (about 20°C/68°F) for 24 hours between each addition.

For the first few days, the mixture might seem lifeless and could smell vinegary or even a bit "off". Don't worry about this, as it should soon start bubbling and the smell will develop into something yeasty and maybe even floral.

Day six (ish)

Once your starter is bubbling up nicely, you can use some to bake a loaf of Real Bread. Typically, this might be anything from four to seven days after you started, but could take a little longer. If it's not bubbling by day six, keep repeating the daily flour and water addition until it is. Don't worry if you end up with a layer of brownish liquid. This is just gravity working its magic and is normal. Either stir it back into your starter or pour it off. If your starter hasn't been used for a while, the second option is probably better as the liquid (sometimes known as "hooch") will have started to become alcoholic, which can slow the starter down and may also lead to less desirable flavours in your bread.

Caring for Your Starter

+ Each time you use some of the starter, simply replace with an equivalent quantity of flour and water – this is usually known as feeding or refreshing. You also need to refresh on the day before a baking session.

+ When refreshing, feel free to experiment with different ratios and total amounts of flour to water: a looser starter will ferment more quickly than a stiff one; refreshing more often or adding a large refreshment will dilute the taste and acidity.

+ It's a living thing (well, technically billions of living things) so get to know it. The acidity, flavour, aromas and speed at which starters work vary, so learn what's normal for yours.

+ Give it a name. You can't call yourself a proper sourdough nut if you don't – though I know some people strongly disagree with me on this one!

+ Forget it. Unlike other members of your household, your starter will be forgiving of neglect. Though it will be happy to help you bake bread once a week or even daily, your starter can be left untouched at the back for the refrigerator for weeks or even months. The yeast and bacteria populations will decline over time but enough will live on in a dormant state. The longer you leave it, the longer it'll take to "wake up" though and it might need a few days' of refreshments before it's up to full vigour.

+ Unless you are using your starter every single day, keep it in the fridge, which will slow it down and reduce the frequency at which you need to refresh it. You just need to remember to take it out and refresh it the day before you intend to make a loaf.

Unnecessary Extras

To make a starter you need nothing but flour and water, but here are some other things you sometimes find in sourdough instructions, along with why that might be:

+ Rhubarb is high in several acids, which can help deter pathogenic (bad) microorganisms and create an environment favoured by lactic acid bacteria.

+ Hops also have anti-bacterial properties.

+ Live yogurt is also acidic and contains lactic acid bacteria, though not necessarily the types most suitable for producing bread.

+ Mashed potato provides an extra source of food for yeast and bacteria.

+ Grapes, raisins, sultanas/golden raisins and so on have yeasts and bacteria on their skins but again,

SOURFAUX

At the time of writing, there is no legal definition for the word "sourdough" and complaints made by the Campaign about products marketed as such, despite being made using baker's yeast and artificial additives, have been dismissed by retailers and the Advertising Standards Authority.

The Real Bread Campaign believes that shoppers seeking genuine sourdough deserve the protection of a definition that only allows the word to be used for loaves made:
• using a live sourdough culture, not inactive dried sourdough powder added purely for taste and acidity

• without the addition of commercial yeast or other leavening agents (e.g. baking powder)
• without any artificial additives
• without any other souring agent (e.g. vinegar or yogurt)

they are not necessarily the strains most suited to making bread.

• Honey is high in sugars, on which the yeast can feed. Unpasteurized honey can also contain yeasts and bacteria.

Enriched dough

If sugars, eggs, dairy products or fats are included, a dough is described as "enriched". These ingredients alter the dough structure and behaviour as well as the character of the finished bread. Enriched doughs require different handling and baking, as sugars and fats interfere with the formation of gluten and have an effect on the speed and temperature at which browning occurs. Examples include brioche, Bath buns and some types of *focaccia*, though others only have oil added after the dough has been made. An enriched dough may be leavened with sourdough culture or commercial yeast.

NB: The added teaspoon of sugar or knob of butter found in some domestic bread recipes does not make them enriched doughs.

Laminated doughs

These differ from enriched doughs in that the fat (e.g. butter, lard or shortening) is added after the dough is made up. The process involves sandwiching the fat between layers of dough, rolling it out, folding to make more layers, then repeating the rolling and folding until the alternating layers of dough and fat are many – and very thin. During baking, the fat melts and both air trapped during folding and carbon dioxide formed by the yeast expand and force the layers apart, to create a flaky structure. Keeping the dough chilled and baking at the right temperature are both essential to ensure the finished product is light and flaky, and not greasy. Examples include croissants, Danish pastries and lardy cake.

BEFORE YOU START

Certain bits of kit and techniques appear in this book over and over again. To save you from having to read the same detail each time, I've collected them together in the following sections on techniques, equipment and ingredients. Please read these notes before setting out on a recipe or you'll forever be saying things like "eh, what does that word mean?" or "hang on, what am I baking this dough on?"

Please also read a recipe from start to finish well before you're thinking of baking it. That's good advice for any recipe but particularly for this book, in which you'll find that the short stages of some recipes are spread over several days.

Throughout the book you'll find suggestions from the experts in the Baker's Tips, as well as additional interesting bits and bobs, which I've called sippets:

Sippet: noun; a small piece of something, for example a piece of toast or fried bread for dipping in soup.

Terms and Techniques

I've tried to keep professional baker speak to a minimum but here are brief explanations of some of the instructions in the book and why you're following them.

Autolyse

This is a word adopted by the late baking expert professor Raymond Calvel for a process of mixing together flour and water and leaving it to rest before adding any other ingredients. Some bakers find it makes mixing and kneading easier and shorter, and improves the structure of their bread. Some bakers wrongly include yeast, but the essential point is not to add the salt until afterward.

Baking times

Baking times depend in part on the weight and type of bread you're making and the oven temperature. For example, if an 800g/1lb 12oz loaf baked at 230°C/210°C fan/450°F/gas 8 takes about 30 minutes, then a 400g/14oz loaf of the same dough might take 22–25 minutes, and 100g/3½oz rolls 15–18 minutes. An enriched dough will require a lower oven temperature as sugars, fruit, butter, milk and some other ingredients colour and burn easily.

Shape will also affect baking time. For example, even if a baguette weighs 400g/14oz, its high surface area to volume ratio would mean the baking time would be less than if baked in a loaf tin or as a cob/boule. Times given are for guidance and you may find a loaf

is baking more quickly or slowly, so keep an eye on it and tweak as appropriate. You might also have to adjust the baking time and/or temperature if you go off-piste and make adjustments to a recipe.

Burst

In the first few minutes of baking, loaves swell rapidly (this is called "oven spring") and can rupture, which is known as a burst. Bursting can be useful in helping to have an open (rather than tight or close) crumb structure, but it can happen at random and not necessarily in an attractive way. For a note on controlling bursting, see Slashing on pages 21–22.

Cleared

A term sometimes used in commercial bakeries, this means that ingredients have been mixed together fully with no dry bits in the bowl or within the dough itself.

Cooling

I've yet to see any evidence to support the notion that bread is more digestible once it has cooled after baking, but there are good reasons for leaving a loaf on a wire rack to cool before slicing. One is that the crumb of newly-baked bread tends not to hold its shape very well and can even be gummy if it is cut before it has cooled. Another is that the loaf will lose a greater amount of moisture as steam if sliced when hot, which can speed drying out and staling.

Cover

This instruction is given several times in every recipe and what you use depends on the situation. If you're proving or resting dough at room temperature, one option is simply to leave it on the work surface and cover with a large mixing bowl. Another is to put the dough into a large bowl and cover with a damp, clean dish towel, large elasticated bowl cover or shower cap. Alternatively, you can slip the bowl into a reusable plastic bag that's large enough to be sealed around it. I try to avoid anything that's single-use, such as cling film/plastic wrap.

Another option is a large plastic container with a sealable lid, which is particularly handy when retarding dough in the fridge. If you're getting more serious and making bread or pizza dough in quantity, stackable dough trays or boxes are the way forward.

Dividing and scaling

If a recipe is for more than one loaf, or is formed from more than one piece (e.g. a plait) you will need to divide the dough. This is best done with your trusty dough scraper (see fig. 1), with the aim of getting it right first time, rather than nibbling bits off one piece to add to the other to even them up.

Ideally, you should check the weight of each piece using electronic scales. Equal weights helps ensure they bake at the same speed, are aesthetically pleasing and, for professional bakers, it is important (or even legally required) that each weighs the same.

Legal Bread Weights

The references to "large" and "small" loaves in this book are just for guidance and don't refer to any standard legal loaf weights. If baking loaves for sale, please check with the relevant authorities in your area for definitive advice on this and for their recommendations on scaling dough to weights that will ensure your baked loaves are within legal limits.

Fermentation

Commonly used to refer to the yeast (and by association, the dough) getting on and doing its thing. Without getting too scientific, yeast cells produce an enzyme that breaks some of the starch in flour down into simpler sugars, which they then metabolize in order to grow and reproduce. One by-product of this is the carbon dioxide that makes dough rise.

Fold

Doing a fold (or a turn, as some bakers call it) has several functions. The two main ones that enthusiastic amateurs need to know are that it helps to develop the gluten in a way that allows for a more open-textured bread; and it redistributes carbon dioxide without totally knocking out those lovely bubbles you've nurtured.

One way to do a fold is to lift the side of the dough furthest from you, gently stretch it upward and then fold it toward you over the rest of the dough. Rotate the dough (or whole bowl, if it's in one) a half turn and repeat the stretch and fold with the side that is now opposite and then do the same for the remaining two sides.

For a double fold, simply repeat this folding process once more.

Heating the oven

Real Bread needs to be baked in an oven that's already hot. If you put it into an oven that's cold or only warm,

the dough will have skinned over by the time it gets up to the right temperature, and your loaf will be far from perfect. To give dough baked in a domestic oven the best chance of getting heat not only by convection from rising hot air, but also radiant heat from the oven walls and heat conducted directly from a baking stone, you should turn the oven on 20–30 minutes (or whatever the oven's manufacturer suggests) before you intend to start baking.

Hydration

This is the amount of liquid (usually water) in relation to flour. A starter or dough using 1kg/2lb 4oz of flour and 700g/1lb 9oz of water would be 70% hydration (I find it much easier to be accurate using metric weights). The lower the percentage, the stiffer the dough (for a bagel or tin loaf, for example) and the higher the percentage, the slacker the dough (great for a ciabatta or crumpet). Very high-hydration doughs can be referred to as batters, though there is no set cut-off point between the two.

Kneading

The process of working the dough to speed the formation and development of the gluten network (see page 26). Like folding, it also helps to even out the bubbles in the dough and redistribute the yeast and – for want of a better analogy – give it a new portion of starch to graze on.

Kneading isn't actually essential. As can be seen from

the no-knead recipes in this book, given enough time and water, the proteins in wheat flour will form gluten of their own accord. Kneading is simply a mechanical means of speeding up this biochemical process.

How Do I Knead?

If you have chosen the kneading route (which can be very therapeutic, after all) please be assured that there's no right or wrong way of doing it. You can turn the mass of dough out onto the work surface, pin down an end with one hand, push the other end away from you with the heel of the other hand (see fig. 1). Bring the dough back together (fig. 2) and repeat (fig. 3). Another way, particularly for softer doughs, is to slap the dough onto the work surface so that one end sticks, pull the other end toward you, fold the dough over on itself, unstick from the work surface and repeat. Just one more of many methods is to take the dough in both hands in the air, stretch it, bring both ends back together and while holding them in one hand take what was the middle of the dough (but is now the other end) in the other and repeat.

In all cases, you'll note that you are repeatedly stretching the dough, folding it over on itself and stretching again.

For How Long Should I Knead?

Until the gluten is fully developed. Sorry I can't just say "for X minutes", but that's how it is. This is because it depends on a range of factors, including the hydration level (i.e. the water-to-flour ratio), temperature and type of dough, as well as how quickly and vigorously you knead – five minutes of a body builder going at it hammer and tongs might be worth ten of someone else's efforts. (See also page 24, on using a mixer.)

So How Do I Know When the Gluten is Properly Developed?

In the early stages, dough tends to be shaggy and sticky, but as it develops it becomes smooth and glossy, with the sticky feeling turning to something that can be described as silky.

An instruction found in some baking books to give an indication of dough development is to do the gluten window or windowpane test. The idea is you knead or work the dough until you can stretch a small section of it out until it is a thin film that you can see light through. This is easiest with a dough made from white wheat strong (bread) flour, harder with higher extraction (i.e. browner), weaker (e.g. plain/all-purpose) or non-wheat flours. A word of caution: a gluten window might not help you to distinguish between a dough that is developed and one that is overdeveloped.

Proving

Proving (some bakers say "proofing") has two meanings in bread making. The less common one is to test that yeast is still active and capable of leavening dough. This is done by either dissolving it in plain water, or in water with a spoonful of sugar or a little flour, to see signs of gas being produced, appearing as bubbles pricking the surface of the mixture after 10–15 minutes. The more common use is to refer to the dough rising, where it sits with several other terms such as "bulk fermentation" (to refer to a large quantity of dough, typically in a commercial bakery, undergoing its first rise after mixing), "second rise" after kneading or being left unkneaded to fully hydrate, and "final proving" (after shaping and just before being baked).

4

Finger Poke Test

When is dough fully proved? This is such a hard question to answer: even if you think you've been precise with every measurement of ingredients, the temperature of the dough and room it's in, time etc., the answer is another case of "when it's done".

One test is pressing gently with a finger or the pad at the base of your thumb (fig. 4). If the dough springs back quickly, it's not ready; if it collapses totally, you've probably left it too long. What you want to see is the dough slowly pushing back to repair the dent you have made. It's one of those things that as you get really serious about your baking, you might want to sidle up to a tame, genuine artisan baker who'll let you poke his or her dough and say "that's what it should feel like".

Release agents

Not always in an ingredients list, but needed more often than not. These are simply things that stop dough sticking, depending on what you are doing:

• During proving: more of whatever flour you're baking with.

• When transferring dough to the oven: professional bakers usually use something more gritty and less absorbent than flour, generally semolina, polenta/cornmeal (although this can burn easily in a very hot oven), or rice cones, which is very coarsely ground rice.

• For preparing tins and trays: professional bakers are split between those that prefer hard fats (lard or hardened vegetable fat – in the quantities they use, butter would get expensive) that can be smeared, or oils (usually a cheap, flavourless vegetable oil) that can be brushed or sprayed.

Recipes in this book generally avoid asking you to throw flour all over work surfaces, as it can change the ingredient ratios, making dough stiffer than it should be, and lead to streaks or unwanted large air pockets in the finished bread. It also makes shaping harder, as you need a slight tackiness, rather than the dough skating around on the surface and against your hands.

Baker's Tip: Use your dough scraper to collect up the semolina, flour etc. you use, sieve it and keep it for dusting in future.

Retarding

Coming from Latin, via French, this means to delay or hold back. Bakers may slow ferment by deliberately proving dough at a lower temperature. In many professional bakeries, this is done in a retarder, but a home baker can use a refrigerator or very cool room. The longer proving time caused by retardation allows for extra flavour development and has an effect on other characteristics of the bread. It also gives the baker greater control over when the dough is ready to be baked.

Room temperature

As this falls into the "how long is a piece of string?" category, let's say ideally it would be about 20°C/68°F. Dough kept below that range will simply prove more slowly, and warmer dough will ferment more quickly.

NB: For consistency, and because they need to stick to a timetable for when loaves need to be baked and ready for sale, professional bakers control the temperature of the dough more carefully. You can read more about this in the Real Bread Campaign's book *Knead to Know*, in professional baking manuals, or by searching online, e.g. for desired dough temperature.

Seam

This is the point at which two or more edges of the dough meet. Typically, you will need to seal them together well by applying pressure, and in some cases use something like water, milk or egg as an adhesive, so that the join doesn't come apart during proving or baking. Most of the recipes in this book also instruct you to bake loaves seam-side down to keep this untidy bit out of sight.

Shape

A key reason for shaping dough carefully, rather than just rolling it into a ragged ball or sausage shape, is to help control its form when proving and baking. This gives you a better chance of avoiding unexpected bursts, or ruptures, which can have a negative impact

on the look and even texture of your Real Bread. This is all much easier if the dough is slightly tacky, so don't add flour or your hands will slip and the loose ends of the dough won't knit together so easily. You also need to try to minimize contact time with the dough at each movement, as the longer your hands are in contact with the dough, the more chance it has to stick to them.

The best way to improve your technique is practice. As you get more serious with your baking, it's also great to take a course with, or work alongside, an experienced baker, so that you can see what they do, copy them, and feel what the dough is doing. He or she will also be able to put you straight if you've not quite got it right.

Many of the loaves in this book are shaped into a ball (to make a boule or cob loaf), or a roughly cylindrical baton, which might end up as a freestanding loaf or in a tin.

Shaping a Ball

Press and stretch the dough out until it's roughly square. Fold the four corners into the centre of the square, and then fold the four new corners into the centre again (fig. 1).

Turn the dough over so that it is seam-side (i.e. the messy bit) down. Starting with your hands side by side and palms down on top of the dough, slide them down round under it, maintaining contact with the dough to create tension in the outer surface

of the dough in the direction your hands are moving. Your hands need to meet underneath the dough, palms up, pinching the dough together between their sides to seal the dough (fig. 2).

Move your hands back to the start position, giving the dough a quarter turn as you do, and repeat. You need to do this several times until you can feel tightness in the dough (if it tears you've overdone it) and the messy bit underneath has sealed together. Place the boule seam-side-up in a floured proving basket (fig. 3), or seam-side-down on a tray.

Shaping a Tin Loaf

Press and stretch the dough out to form a rectangle about the same length of your loaf tin, with the long side closest to you. Hold your hands flat, palms facing towards you, with the fingers touching. Put them under the edge furthest from you to lift and fold about a quarter of the dough towards you (fig. 4).

As you fold the far edge over, use the lower side of your hands to push the dough from you slightly to create tension on the outer surface and pinch it down (fig. 5). Return your hands behind the dough and repeat these steps once or twice more to pinch the seam closed. Carefully place the dough, seam-side down, into the greased bread tin (fig. 6).

Slashing

As well as looking pretty, at one time acting as a baker's (or dough owner's, in the case of communal ovens) signature and helping to distinguish between different types of bread baked in the same shape, scoring the dough serves technical functions. One is to control where the dough bursts (splits) during the rapid expansion in the first stage of baking. Encouraging and controlling this burst also leads to a better, less tight, texture of the finished loaf.

Slashing should be done in a swift, clean, decisive stroke with a very sharp blade, just before you put a loaf into the oven. Using a blunt knife, sawing back and forth, snagging the dough, stabbing away aggressively, having multiple attempts, barely breaking the surface, or doing any of this before the end of the final proof won't get you anywhere.

Steam

Unless otherwise stated, the Real Breads in this book will benefit from steam in the first 5–10 minutes of baking. Steam turns the outer surface of the dough into a flexible gel, which allows it to expand more easily than if a dry crust starts forming straight away. Later in the dry heat stage of baking this gel sets to form a shiny, and in some cases crackly, crust.

In a fully-loaded traditional bread oven, steam is generated by evaporation from the dough and many professional bread ovens allow the baker to inject steam. At home it can be a struggle as domestic ovens are rarely airtight and may even have a fan to extract the steamy air. Still, you can give it a go by putting a tray in the bottom of the oven and pouring a small amount of boiling water from the kettle into it shortly before loading the dough in. Some bakers suggest squirting a mist of water into the oven immediately before you close the door. Try one of those trigger spray bottles you can buy in garden centres – a new one, not one that's been used for plant food or pesticide . . .

Testing that a loaf is fully baked

I'm afraid that the old "knock on the bottom and if it sounds hollow, it's done" trick, doesn't really work. A more scientific method is to use a temperature probe – the general rule is that it should be 95°C/205°F at the centre.

Turn

Most ovens have spots that are hotter than others. It's a good idea to turn loaves through 180 degrees at least once during baking to ensure even browning. For another meaning of "turn", see Fold on page 17.

Weighing and measuring

You'll notice that everything in this book is measured first by weight, and secondarily by volume. This is for accuracy and consistency. Depending on how much it is compacted, quantities of flour and other dry ingredients can vary hugely from cup to cup, and a jug at a slight tilt can lead to the amount of liquid you think it contains being way out. The cup measure of a starter will also vary depending on how active and bubbly it is. I suggest buying electronic kitchen scales and getting comfortable with metric weights.

That said, if you are comfortable and experienced in baking using ounces or cups, by all means continue to do what feels right to you. And remember: bakers often have to make slight adjustments to recipes (to account for the absorbency of different flours, for example) and when you've tried baking something once, you might want to tweak relative amounts of ingredients to make it your own. Still, weighing in grams is a useful fixed point of reference from which you can then go exploring.

All recipes in this book were written and tested using metric measurements. Conversions to ounces or cups are rounded and may be approximate: for example, in a list of ingredients, 500g will convert to 1lb 2oz, but when equipment is being discussed, the convention is to refer to a 500g/1lb loaf tin.

Equipment

When you think about it, the things you actually need to make Real Bread are few. The only truly essential bits of kit for making most Real Bread are your hands, a work surface, an oven and something to put the dough in or on for baking. But we don't wear hair shirts, and this isn't the Stone Age, so here are some non-essential (but very handy) bits of kit, which are all available from various cooking or baking equipment shops and websites. How many of these you choose to get your mitts on is up to you.

Baking sheets

If you're not using a baking stone, you'll need a heavy gauge stainless steel or anodized aluminium baking sheet (and preferably several) for freestanding loaves. The thicker the sheet the better, as thin sheets can buckle with the heat of the oven. At home, you might find it convenient to line it with baking parchment, though in a professional bakery they usually rely on good greasing to ensure the dough comes away easily.

Baking stone

The clue's in the name – it's a bit of stone on which to bake. Opinion is divided, but many domestic bakers swear by using one. That's because it helps to imitate the masonry sole (floor) of a professional oven, which stores up heat then releases it up through the dough during baking to give a hefty oven spring, helping loaves reach their full potential volume. Of course, a baking stone can't store up and deliver anything like the heat that a thick slab of brick or refractory

concrete can, but it'll be more than you'll get from a flimsy baking sheet. I suggest you seek out the thickest baking stone you can find, ideally 2.5cm/1in thick or more. Place it on the centre shelf of your oven before you turn it on to heat up for baking.

Blade

Tools that can be used to slash loaves must be very sharp and include straight or scalloped (but not serrated) knives, a baker's lame (it rhymes with farm: similar to a razor blade) held in a tool called a grignette, or even an actual razor blade. If using the latter, a dirt cheap grignette can be made using one of those wooden stirrers found in coffee shops. Whatever you use, please be sure to keep your fingers safe from deep and painful cuts, when fixing the blade or slashing the dough.

Casserole dish

A cast iron cooking pot or cast aluminium Dutch oven with a lid can be used to approximate the conditions of a professional oven by trapping steam and providing plenty of both bottom and radiated heat to the loaf. Put both pot and lid in the oven when you turn it on, then remove the lid after the first 10–15 minutes of baking, or when specified by a recipe.

Couche

This is a stiff, coarse cloth, usually made from natural fibre such as linen or hemp. Folded into

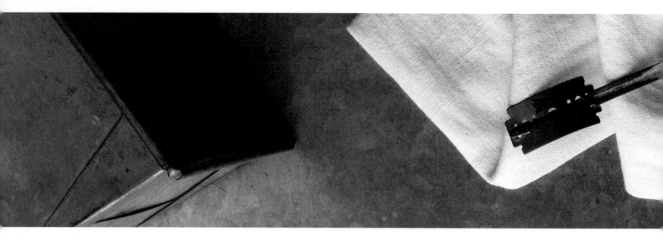

ridges, and dusted with flour, it is used to hold softer doughs (e.g. baguettes) in shape while proving and it is also used to line some types of proving baskets. As with proving baskets, keep them dry, clean and don't wash them.

Dough scraper

I recommend you buy a flexible, plastic scraper: it's one of the cheapest and best bread-making purchases you can make. For many bakers, a scraper becomes an extension of the hand. It can be used to mix and divide dough, lift it out of the bowl or off a work surface, and to scrape any scraps or dried bits off bowls, hands and work surfaces when cleaning up.

Loaf tins

Unless you're going freestanding loaves all the way, invest in a heavy-gauge loaf tin (or "loaf pan", in the US) or three – one that will hold a 1kg/2lb loaf, and a couple of 500g/1lb ones would be a good place to start. A deep-walled, good quality metal tin will give excellent results and a traditionally shaped loaf. Always use a release agent (see pages 19–20) to ensure loaves don't stick. Pay particular attention to the corners and the neck (i.e. top part) of the tin.

If your loaf doesn't come out of the tin easily after baking, leave it for a few minutes and then try again, as steam coming off the loaf can help to release it. If it still sticks, use the straight edge of a plastic dough scraper to release the edges. Don't be tempted to use a knife as you could puncture your loaf or scratch the sides of the tin.

Mixer

For most people, kneading by hand is part of the fun and therapy of bread making. Still, if you have a powerful mixer, there's no reason you shouldn't break out its dough hook – it'll be particularly handy for high-hydration doughs like focaccia and ciabatta. With a few exceptions who feel that "made by hand" should include mixing and kneading, almost all professional bakers use a dough mixer. A word of warning, many domestic food mixers aren't suitable for bread making and you risk burning out the motor.

Mixing bowl

You can mix straight on a table or work surface, but a bowl comes in handy. Something like a 3 litre/ 100fl oz/14 cup bowl is a good size for mixing and proving up to 1kg/2lb 4oz of dough.

Oven

All of these recipes assume you'll be baking in a domestic oven, which hopefully will get up to somewhere approaching 250°C/500°F.

Oven temperatures

All of the recipes in this book were based on metric temperatures with approximate conversions into Fahrenheit and gas marks.

Peel

A baker's peel is a bit like a flat shovel, usually wooden, used to transfer freestanding dough into the oven. You could use a bit of hardboard/Masonite, or even thick, non-corrugated cardboard – for years I just used the disc that came in a pizza box. Before placing dough onto it, dust it well with semolina, polenta/cornmeal, coarse ground rice or flour.

Proving basket

Known as a *banneton* in French and *brotform* in German, as the name suggests this is a basket, usually made of cane or wood pulp (there's a company in the UK that makes recycled plastic ones), used to hold dough in shape while it's proving. Without it, slacker dough would spread out. They also have the advantage of being stackable and in some cases making nice patterns on the crust.

An alternative is a bowl lined with well-floured linen, although as this doesn't allow the dough to "breathe", condensation can build up and make the floury cloth sticky.

Proving baskets shouldn't be washed but should be brushed to remove flour and allowed to dry before storage or they can attract mould.

Scales

As noted in the Weighing and Measuring section on page 22, I recommend you use metric measurements for all your baking, and invest in a set of electronic kitchen scales.

Thermometers

If you are really serious about your baking, there are a couple of different sorts of thermometers that will come in handy.

Dough Thermometer

Ideally of the digital probe variety, though that's a bit of a luxury item for the home baker, this will enable you to check that your loaf has reached 95°C/205°F at the centre. Professional bakers who need absolute accuracy to keep to production schedules also use a thermometer to test the temperature of the water and also the finished but unbaked dough.

Oven Thermometer

Thermostats on domestic ovens tend to be inaccurate, so an oven thermometer is useful to ensure your oven is at the temperature it says it is.

Wire racks

You will usually need to turn a loaf out of its baking tin as soon as it finishes baking and leave it to cool on a rack, or the bottom will "sweat" and go soggy. If you don't have a wire rack, use something similar that will allow air to circulate under the loaf, like the rack from a grill/broiler pan or a (cool) shelf from the oven, safely raised a little above the level of the work surface underneath it.

Ingredients

As a domestic baker, you might be used to simply grabbing a bag labelled "bread flour" or "strong white flour", and sachets of fast-action dried yeast. As your baking develops, you might want to think and learn more about what you're baking with, so here are some points to set you off on that path. There are many ingredients that can be used when making Real Bread but here are some notes on the main ones.

Organic ingredients

Organic and biodynamic farming both have less reliance on herbicides, fungicides, pesticides and petrochemical fertilizers than so-called "conventional" farming. Some organic and biodynamic farmers use none of these substances. This results in a lower negative (and in some cases, an actual positive) impact on the health of the soil and surrounding water systems, and means lower levels of potentially toxic residues in the food chain. It's also possible that the populations of yeasts and lactic acid bacteria that you need for your sourdough starter will be more abundant in flour milled from grain that hasn't been doused in fungicide. Look for research published by academic, governmental and organic food organizations for other possible and proven benefits of organic food production.

Artificial additives

A loaf made using artificial additives, as defined by food regulations, is not what the Campaign calls Real Bread. If you find a recipe elsewhere that instructs you to throw any into your dough, I'd suggest that you find another recipe. After all, could supposed quick or easy fixes peddled by baking "ingredients" companies hold you back from increasing your skills as a baker even further?

FLOUR

This is the main ingredient of Real Bread and the most important building block of your loaf. Most of the recipes in this book are made with wheat flour.

Gluten

A large percentage of the protein in wheat flour is gluten, though gluten isn't a single substance, it is formed by the combinations of two groups of proteins: glutenin and gliadin.

+ **Glutenin** is elastic (i.e. tends to spring back to its original shape) and gives strength.

+ **Gliadin** is plastic (i.e. extensible) and sticky.

If you looked under a powerful microscope, you'd see that gluten is made up of coiled-up strands that look like mini springs. As the gluten develops, the strands begin to uncoil and start to form links to other strands close by, joining together to form what looks like a net. As this microscopic mesh develops, forming more and more links, it becomes like bubble gum, able to trap gas. This stretchy network of gluten strands is the main building material of the walls of the holes we see in wheat bread.

Strength

Many of these recipes specify strong flour. This means wheat flour with a relatively high percentage of the proteins that combine to form gluten. The characteristic lower height and large, uneven crumb structure cells in certain continental-style breads are achieved in part by using flours with lower and/or weaker protein, which is less elastic and so stretches out, and in places the walls between cells (the holes or bubbles) will break down to form larger ones.

If you want to move your baking up a gear, it's worth trying to find millers or flour suppliers willing to give you advice on the appropriate flour to use to achieve particular results, or suitable for the characteristics of the type of bread you are trying to make.

Extraction rate

This is the term used for the proportion or percentage of the de-husked and cleaned wheat grain (also known as the wheat berry) that makes it into the flour sack and is expressed as a percentage. Wholemeal/wholewheat flour should be 100% extraction (though see the note below on stone-ground vs. roller-milled flour); British-milled white bread flour will be around 75%, and brown flour will fall somewhere in between, usually 80–85%.

Continental millers use different systems of classification, based on how much ash is left when the flour is incinerated under controlled conditions. The higher the number, the more ash, indicating higher fibre. Just to make things more confusing, each country's systems differ from each other.

Stone me!

Most of our bread flour is milled using high-speed, fluted steel rollers. Modern roller milling is ruthlessly efficient at stripping away the nutrient-rich germ and fibrous outer layers of cereal grains, separating them into many different fractions and leaving behind a white powder that's not much more than starch and gluten. Millers in the UK are required by law to add certain minerals and vitamins (namely calcium, iron and vitamins B_1 and B_3) to all white bread flour, however it has been produced. Similar additions are required in other countries.

The "wholemeal/wholewheat" flour produced by roller mills is in fact an attempt at reconstructing 100% extraction flour by recombining the bran and wheatgerm with the white flour. Though in the UK wholemeal flour has to contain all of the fractions in their original proportions by law, we have been told a number of times by people in the milling industry who do not want to be named that this is not always the case. For example, a roller-miller might exclude the nutrient-rich and flavoursome germ.

By contrast, stone milling grinds all parts of the grain together, and the process of achieving different extraction rates is reversed: wholemeal/wholewheat flour is the natural end product, which has to be sieved to remove bran to produce whiter flours. Even when sieved, stoneground flour will still contain some fine particles of the fibrous and most nutritious parts – the germ and bran.

Artificial additives

When purchasing flour, always check the ingredients list to make sure that the mill has not added any "improvers" or other non-mandatory artificial additives.

Local loaves

Is there an independent mill in your area? By using their flour you will forge a personal link in the chain from seed to sandwich, help to support local employment and the local economy, and minimize the energy used in transporting the flour. If it is a traditional wind- or water-powered mill, the energy used in milling will be non-polluting and you will be supporting local heritage. Better still is if the grain has been grown as locally as possible, too.

THE WHEAT FAMILY

Rather than being just one type of grain, wheat is a whole family (the genus *Triticum*) of species and sub species. While varieties of common or bread wheat (*Triticum aestivum*) account for over 90% of world wheat production, other cultivated wheats include:

- **Durum wheat** (*T. durum* or *T. turgidum durum*) is commonly used for pasta, but also for some types of bread.

- **Einkorn** (*T. monococcum*) was one of the first domesticated cereals.

- **Emmer** (*T. dicoccum*), sometimes called farro (e.g. in Tuscany), was another of the first domesticated cereals, though probably later than einkorn.

- **Kamut** is a trademarked brand name for one variety of khorasan – see below.

- **Khorasan** (*T. turanicum* or *T. turgidum* subsp. *turanicum*) is a high-protein wheat, originally thought to have been bred in ancient Egypt.

- **Spelt** (*T. spelta* or *T. aestivum* var. *spelta*) is apparently becoming ever-more popular, particularly for bread making.

None of the above are gluten free, and so they are not suitable for people with coeliac disease. That said, there are differences between the make-up of their gluten and that of bread wheat. Some people with a professionally diagnosed allergy or an intolerance (neither of which is the same as coeliac disease, which is an auto-immune condition) to bread wheat report that they have fewer, or no, problems digesting products made from other members of the wheat family. There are also suggestions that the older wheats above may have higher levels of certain micronutrients (vitamins and minerals) than modern bread wheats. The same may go for older varieties (or cultivars) of *T. aestivum*, sometimes known as heritage wheats.

Flour classification

Different countries have their own systems for classifying flour, and types from one country are not always directly comparable with those from another. For example, taking two flours classified by extraction rate (i.e. the percentage of the whole grain it contains after sifting) or ash content (the residue left after controlled incineration), one might have been made from soft wheats, whose lower gluten content is good for cakes and pastries, and the other from hard wheats with higher gluten content more suitable for bread making or even pasta.

Here are the types of wheat flour used in this book:

- **Bread or strong** (British): made from hard wheats, often grown in the USA or Canada. Typically 12–14% protein and an extraction rate of around 75% (white), 80–85% (brown) and 100% (wholemeal). Roughly comparable to US bread flour.

- **Plain** (British): made from soft wheats, often grown in Britain, with less gluten. Typically 8–11% protein and 50–70% extraction. Roughly comparable to US all-purpose flour.

- **T55** (French): made from hard and soft wheats, often grown in France, with an intermediate gluten content. Typically 10–12% protein and 75–78% extraction.

- **T65** (French): made from hard and soft wheats, often grown in France, also with an intermediate gluten content. Typically 10–11.5% protein and 80% extraction, so slightly darker than T55.

- **Tipo 00** (Italian): very white; if intended for bread making, it is usually made from common wheat (*grano tenero*), often grown in Italy. Typically 7–9% protein and around 50% extraction. Tipo 00 made with durum wheat (*grano duro*) is more suitable for pasta.

- **Tipo 1** (Italian): made from soft wheats, often grown in Italy. Typically 10% protein and around 80% extraction, so into brown flour territory.

And this is all before you take into account how it's been milled or how coarsely . . .

For more information, the Internet is your friend. There are stacks of articles, forum posts and blogs with suggestions for substituting one flour for another, so happy browsing – and experimenting.

Other flours

There are many other flours that can be used to make Real Bread, though they won't give the same results as wheat flour, because in general, they lack the necessary gluten. Here are those used in this book.

Chestnut

Not to be confused with the bitter horse chestnut (*Aesculus hippocastanum*), sweet chestnuts (*Castanea sativa*) can be milled to produce flour. Unsurprisingly, its flavour is nutty and slightly sweet, but being gluten free, it needs combining with wheat or other flours if you want to use it to make a risen loaf.

Buckwheat

Despite the name, it isn't a type of wheat. Buckwheat (*Fagopyrum esculentum*) is in fact related to sorrel and rhubarb. As it's not a cereal but is often used like one, it is known as a pseudocereal. While its nutritional profile is very good – high levels of protein, micronutrients and bioflavonoids – as a gluten-free flour it's more suited to flatbreads, pancakes and noodles than risen loaves. For bread, it really benefits from being mixed with wheat flour.

Oats

In his dictionary, Dr. Samuel Johnson noted oats (*Avena sativa*) as being "a grain, which in England is generally given to horses, but in Scotland supports the people". A tad harsh on both Scots and oats, especially as the latter are nutritious and delicious.

The gumminess you see in porridge/oatmeal is generated by beta-glucans in the oats which can also be used to help create structure in bread, though oat flour is better suited to flatbreads unless mixed with wheat or other flours. Beta-glucans are a form of soluble fibre that has been shown to reduce blood cholesterol levels.

On the coeliac disease front, oats contain the protein avenin, which can trigger the coeliac response in some sufferers. In addition, oat cultivation and processing can be contaminated with wheat and other gluten-containing cereals unless certified otherwise.

Rye

Cultivated from the Neolithic era in Turkey, and in Europe since the Bronze Age, rye (*Secale cereale*) is a relative of wheat in the biological tribe *Triticeae*. While it has protein levels similar to those of wheat and contains secalin, a gliadin-like protein that makes it unsuitable for people with coeliac disease, it is low in glutenin and therefore has a lower gluten-forming potential than wheat flour. Much of the structure in 100% rye bread comes from its starch and substances called pentosan gums.

A loaf made with 100% rye flour, low hydration and baker's yeast tends to be a sad, pasty affair: you really need to go for a longer-fermented, high-hydration sourdough to bring this grain alive!

Rye flour is either referred to as wholegrain (or dark, i.e. 100% extraction), or, if it has been sifted (and perhaps bleached in some countries), as light. With exceptions such as Germany, there isn't always the same consistency of classification as with wheat flour.

A hybrid of wheat and rye is called triticale, which is in limited cultivation as a commercial crop.

YEAST

Yeasts are microscopic, single-celled fungi. Yeast cells occur naturally and are all around us in the air and on other living things, like cereal grains.

NB: When making a sourdough starter, it's the latter that's important, so ignore any assertion that you need to leave your mixture of flour and water uncovered, or take it outside, in order to "catch" yeast from the air.

Like people, yeast cells use carbohydrates for energy to live. In bread making, yeasts produce enzymes that break the starch in the flour into simpler sugars upon which they can feed – you don't need to add any extra! Two key by-products of this process are carbon dioxide and alcohol, both of which are involved to a greater or lesser extent in bread making, brewing and winemaking.

Commercial yeast

When bakers (and brewers, for that matter) talk about yeast, they're usually referring to one species, *Saccharomyces cerevisiae*, which takes its name from ancient Greek and Latin words related to sugar, fungus and beer.

The process of cultivating and purifying *S. cerevisiae* commercially was first developed in the mid-19th century. Later on, scientists bred different strains of this species for specific characteristics, including fast production of large volumes of carbon dioxide (for bread making), production of alcohol (for drinks production) and particular flavour profiles (for brewing and winemaking though, interestingly, not for bread making).

Dried yeast

Dried active yeast should be just the same as fresh yeast, just with more water removed. Instant (also known as fast acting, easy blend or easy bake) yeast is used in smaller amounts and, as the name suggests, generates carbon dioxide more quickly.

A word of warning: most brands of both dried active and instant yeast we've found in the UK contain one or more artificial additives. It is for this reason that I have chosen to specify fresh yeast throughout this book for the non-sourdough recipes. Given the processes that might be used by some "conventional" yeast producers, you might also wish to choose yeast produced by a certified organic producer.

Yeast Conversions

If you find an additive-free brand of dried active yeast, or simply can't get hold of fresh, then calculate the amount you need by dividing a recipe's fresh yeast weight in half. If you find an additive-free brand of instant yeast (good luck!), then dividing the fresh yeast recipe weight by three is about right. Note that these calculations don't hold exactly true if baking in quantity so, as ever, have an experiment to see what happens.

Barmy army

While continental European bakers largely continued their traditions of sourdough bread making, British bakers long saw any hint of sourness as a fault. Instead, they turned to brewers for the copious amounts of yeast-rich foam, known as barm, produced during beer making. Even though a commercial yeast process had been developed in Austria-Hungary in the late 1840s, British bakers continued with barm for much longer – references to "pints of yeast" in bakers' manuals can be found into the 20th century. While this book doesn't have a barm bread recipe, it does have one using trub, the yeast at the bottom of a brewing vessel (see page 46).

Sourdough starter

Sourdough is in this section because it contains yeast. Anyone who tells you different is a) wrong and b) potentially breaking the law if they're marketing sourdough loaves as "yeast free".

SALT

As a Tuscan baker may tell you, salt isn't an essential ingredient in bread making, but frankly a loaf made without it will be a bit bland to most people's taste.

Salt also:

+ Strengthens the gluten network, helping the structure of your loaf.

+ Aids the browning process – bread with very low levels of salt may appear paler than loaves made otherwise identically, while high levels may cause loaves to have a reddish, "foxy" bloom to the crust.

+ Acts as a natural preservative, delaying the onset of mould growth.

+ Slows fermentation, though using salt as the "brakes" in home baking is never necessary: lower temperature and lower levels of yeast will help you keep your dough under control.

You might want to choose salt produced by a small, independently owned business that provides more work per kilo for local people than an industrial producer does. You might also find certain brands have processing methods (e.g. sun-drying of sea water) that use less energy and generate lower negative environmental impacts.

Salt and health

Current government guidelines in the UK are that adults shouldn't consume more than 6g of salt a day. They also say that bread should have no more than 1% salt as a percentage of the baked loaf weight.

This guideline applies to professional bakers but you might want to consider them when baking at home. In the end, how much salt you use is up to you but you can read more about the related health issues at actiononsalt.org.uk and worldactiononsalt.com.

FATS AND OILS

Fats and oils are only used in this book when they are necessary to help create the particular taste and texture of an enriched dough. Please consider sticking to the type of fat specified as they were chosen for good reason. Ultimately, though, if you have a religious, cultural or ethical reason for not eating animal fat, it's up to you if you want to make a substitution.

Fats and oils added in appropriate amounts can also be used to do a number of things in a loaf. These include creating a softer crust and crumb, making your bread moister, increasing how stretchy your dough is (and so allowing greater volume) and slowing the effects of staling. Using too much or too little will defeat the object, though, and at least some of these effects can be achieved in other ways, not least by adding a bit more water instead. Give it a go and see what you think.

SUGARS

Refined sugar, honey and syrups are also only used in this book when they are necessary to help create the particular taste and texture of an enriched dough.

For any recipe you see elsewhere that includes one form or other of sugar, ask why. If it is a good reason, in terms of flavour or texture, then go ahead. If it is a savoury loaf, then do you really need that extra sugar in your diet? Remember, yeast doesn't need sugar to feed on, as flour provides more than enough energy to keep it going.

Troubleshooting

Don't Panic!

There will be times when things don't go quite the way you'd expected but don't worry – this happens to the world's best bakers. Though some industrial loaf fabricators may beg to differ, baking isn't an endlessly replicable chemistry experiment. It involves working with natural ingredients with natural variations, which you'll be doing in a domestic kitchen that, at a guess, isn't a computer-controlled industrial loaf production unit.

Printed recipes are always limited by having to describe in words some things that can only be explained by hands-on experience; even visual media – photos, diagrams or video – have limitations. Really, the best way to learn and improve your loaf-making skills, and how to put things right when they go wrong, is by spending time alongside a skilled baker. If you're keen on this baking malarkey, then we recommend taking a bread-making class or course (or two: all bakers do things differently and you'll learn something from each), where your tutor will be able to say "here, feel this dough" and your hands will let you know and understand what the phrase "kneaded enough" or "fully proved" actually means.

But, we're here in this book together, so let's have a go at a few of the more common things that might not work out and some of the most likely causes.

Dough doesn't rise enough

Not Enough Water

Bread recipes in some domestic baking books produce low-hydration doughs: that is, they have relatively high flour to water ratios. This will be exacerbated if a "stickyphobe" baker throws armfuls of flour around to dust the work surface, dough and hands during production. Such "tight" doughs will be less stretchy than doughs that have a higher proportion of water. As Andrew Whitley says, "the wetter the better!"

Not Enough Time

A recipe isn't a law: baking is as much an art as a science. Just because one recipe says the second proof for a particular loaf is two hours, doesn't mean you must put it in the oven after 120 minutes, regardless of whether or not it's ready to bake. If you don't think the dough has risen enough, give it a while longer.

The baked bread is deformed

Poor Shaping/Moulding

Professional bakers don't just roll dough into balls and chuck them in bread tins: they mould it carefully to create an invisible structure of tension around and within. See Shape on pages 20–21.

Under-Proved

Dough that's put in the oven before it's fully proved will expand in the first few minutes of baking much more quickly and unpredictably. This can cause it to bulge unevenly or even burst in places you didn't want it to.

Over-Proved

Conversely, dough that's been left to ferment too long can collapse when baked.

Poor Slashing

If you're slashing, each stroke should be done in a single, decisive movement. Sawing backwards and forwards will deflate your loaf and make a mess, and if the cut is too shallow it won't create an adequate "fault line" of weakness and the burst will happen elsewhere.

Loaf very heavy/dense

A loaf that's fluffy and really large for its weight might suggest that the baker has used artificial additives to achieve this, and so a denser loaf can be taken as one sign (though not a guarantee), that it's Real Bread: but nobody wants to be eating a brick, so consider the following possibilities:

Higher Fibre Flours

Bran interferes with gluten development, partly because it means that the percentage by weight of the flour that can form gluten is lower than in white flour, and partly because flakes of it create physical barriers to gluten strands forming and cross-linking.

Over-Enriched

Oils, fats and sugars all interfere with gluten development. Use too much and the loaf won't rise properly. One technique that can help is to make the flour, water and yeast into a dough first, to get the gluten development underway before adding the enriching ingredients.

Under-Proved

Putting dough into the oven before it's ready will result in a heavier loaf. Next time, allow to prove for longer or adjust the amount of yeast you use or raise the proving temperature. Of the three, the first is preferable.

Under/Poorly Baked

If your oven is too cool for the type of dough you're baking and/or you don't leave it in long enough, it won't bake through properly. Your loaf might not only be dense, it could also be raw in the centre. If on the other hand your oven is too hot for that type of dough, it could bake or even burn (a particular risk with enriched doughs) on the outside before it's cooked through. Some professional bakers use dough thermometers to be sure that loaves are fully baked at the centre.

Retarded Dough Not Left to Warm

If you retard your dough, you must take it out of the refrigerator and leave it long enough to get back up to, or above, ambient temperature before baking.

Pre-Ferment

Biga, sponge and dough, poolish; the list of members of the pre-ferment family just goes on.

A pre-ferment is made from flour, water and yeast left to ferment for a number of hours, perhaps overnight. It is then added to the bulk of the dough's other ingredients.

There are several reasons Real Bread bakers may choose to do this. One is that it allows less or weaker strains of yeast to be used. Another is that it can help build gluten strength and stretchiness; particularly useful when working with softer, weaker flours.

Key considerations also include that a pre-ferment helps to develop compounds that will boost the flavour and aroma of the finished loaf.

The yeast in a pre-ferment can be from a sourdough starter but for the purposes of this book, the recipes in this chapter are mainly made using baker's yeast.

Brown Bread MARK WOODS

A supermarket "brown bread" label doesn't tell you much, other than it ain't wholemeal/wholewheat, but it ain't white either. The bran and wheat germ content could be minimal and it might be coloured with caramel to give it a more pleasing or apparently wholesome appearance. Mark's recipe brings back brown Real Bread as an honest loaf that can be part of a healthier diet, and is also a stepping stone to wholemeal/wholewheat for some kids.

MAKES: 1 large or 2 small loaves
FROM MIXING TO OVEN: 12–16 hours, or overnight plus 4–5 hours
BAKING TIME: 45 minutes

FOR THE PRE-FERMENT:
250g/9oz/1¾ cups white bread flour
350g/12oz/1½ cups warm water
2g/scant ½ tsp fresh yeast

FOR THE DOUGH:
100g/3½oz/¾ cup minus ½ tbsp white bread flour
150g/5½oz/1 cup wholemeal/wholewheat bread flour
5g/1 tsp fresh yeast
5g/1 tsp fine/table salt

butter or oil, for greasing (optional)

1. Mix the pre-ferment ingredients together thoroughly until you have a sloppy batter. Cover and leave in the refrigerator for 8–12 hours or overnight.

2. Add the dough ingredients to the pre-ferment and mix until there are no dry patches of flour, then knead the dough until smooth and stretchy. Cover and leave to rise at room temperature for about 2 hours, giving the dough a fold after the first 20, 40 and 60 minutes.

3. Grease a 1kg/2lb loaf tin (or two 500g/1lb tins for small loaves) or dust a large proving basket with flour. Shape the dough to fit and place it seam-side down in the tin or seam-side up in the basket. Cover and leave to rise at room temperature for a further 2 hours. Heat the oven to 240°C/220°C fan/475°F/gas 8–9 with a baking stone or baking sheet in place if you are letting the dough rise in a basket.

4. Either place the loaf tin in the oven, or carefully turn the dough out of the proving basket onto a well-floured peel and slide it onto the baking stone. Bake for about 45 minutes.

Mark Woods is a psychiatric nurse by day. In his free time, he runs the Slow Loaf microbakery and baking school in the West Midlands town of Walsall. He says, "We are losing so much in our fast-paced world. I am passionate about passing on my bread skills to anyone that will listen, teaching as many classes as possible throughout the year."

White Bread with Old Dough

SHEILA TUSKAN SAGER

MAKES: 1 large loaf

FROM MIXING TO OVEN: overnight plus 2–3 hours

BAKING TIME: 30 minutes

Old dough is the British version of what the French call *pâte fermentée*. The fermentation it has undergone means it helps to boost flavour, and it was once common for bakers to use it in what were called "short process" breads, to help them develop truly great character and texture.

3g/¾ tsp fresh yeast
500g/1lb 2oz/3½ cups white bread flour
320g/11¼oz/1⅓ cups water
8g/1½ tsp fine/table salt
200g/7oz old dough

1. Rub the yeast into the flour, then mix in most of the water. Knead the dough until the ingredients come together and no dry patches remain, adding more water if the dough seems too stiff or any floury patches remain. It's better to err on the side of what might seem too wet at this stage.

2. Cover the dough and leave it to relax for 15 minutes. Sprinkle the salt over the dough and knead for a minute or two until it is evenly mixed in.

3. Break the old dough into small pieces, scatter them over the fresh dough and knead until they are full incorporated. Depending on how vigorous a kneader you are, it could take anything from 8–15 minutes.

4. Put the dough into a bowl, cover and leave in the refrigerator overnight, taking it out about 2 hours before you plan to bake. If you plan to make this recipe again in a few days, cut off 200g/7oz of the dough and keep it in a container in the refrigerator, to use as the old dough next time. Shape the loaf as desired, cover it and leave it to rise at room temperature for about 2 hours.

5. Heat the oven to 200°C/180°C fan/400°F/gas 6, with a baking stone or baking sheet in place. Using a floured peel, transfer the dough onto the baking stone and bake for about 30 minutes.

Baker's Tip: The old dough can be a bit left over from any type of bread, kept in the fridge in a sealed container for up to four days.

Sheila Tuskan Sager began baking Real Bread in 1997. Having given up a career as a construction manager to relocate to the UK, Sheila decided to spend her new-found free time learning the science behind bread. By keeping ingredients to the basics of flour, water, salt and a tiny amount of baker's yeast, she quickly discovered that the longer the bread was fermented, the better the flavour. This fact inspired the bread that she and her team made at the Shrewsbury Bakehouse.

Buckwheat and Chia Bread

CHRIS STAFFERTON

Chia seed and psyllium husk help provide structure for this wheat- and gluten-free Real Bread dough. The mucilage in each of these natural ingredients works with the starches to trap fermentation gases, and enable the dough to rise.

MAKES: 1 loaf

FROM MIXING TO OVEN: 12–13 hours, or overnight plus 4–5 hours

BAKING TIME: 35–40 minutes

1. Mix the pre-ferment ingredients together, cover and leave at room temperature for about 8 hours, or in the refrigerator overnight.

2. Gently mix all of the dry dough ingredients into the pre-ferment, using a whisk to ensure there are no lumps, then gradually work in as much of the water as you need to produce a stiff but shapeable dough. Cover the dough and leave to rise at room temperature for 2 hours.

3. Dust a round proving basket well with buckwheat flour. Shape the dough into a ball (unlike wheat dough, the absence of gluten means it won't stretch in the way you are used to) and place this in the basket. Cover and leave to rise at room temperature for a further 2 hours.

4. Heat the oven to 220°C/200°C fan/425°F/gas 7, with a baking stone or baking sheet in place. Turn the dough out onto a floured peel and slash the top, to control the way the dough expands and to avoid unusual bursts in the crust. Slide the dough onto the baking stone and bake for 35–40 minutes.

FOR THE PRE-FERMENT:

150g/5½oz/1¼ cups buckwheat flour

150g/5½oz/scant ⅔ cup water

2g/scant ½ tsp fresh yeast

FOR THE DOUGH:

200g/7oz/1⅓ cups buckwheat flour

15g/½oz/1 tbsp ground chia seeds/ chia meal

15g/½oz/1 tbsp psyllium husks

4g/¾ tsp salt

200g/7oz/¾ cup plus 1 tbsp water

Chris Stafferton started baking bread occasionally in the late 1970s. Nearly 30 years later his doctor told him to learn to live without gluten. Finding the available gluten-free bread terrible, he set out to develop naturally gluten-free Real Bread. Through his website he sells gluten-free recipes and online tuition around the world.

Robert Swift is a fifth-generation baker at Swifts Bakery, started over 150 years ago by his great-great-great-aunt in Wheaton Aston, Staffordshire. He says, "We pride ourselves on doing things properly, no matter what we are producing." In addition to running six shops and a wholesale business, he and his brother offer baking courses that promote how Real Bread should be made.

Stromboli ROBERT SWIFT

Perhaps it's the molten cheese spilling like lava from the slashes in the top of the loaf that prompted someone to name this filled, Italian-style dough after the island with an active volcano north of Sicily. Then again, maybe it's named after the 1950s Ingrid Bergman film of the same name. What seems certain is that it springs from Italian-American cuisine, rather than from Italy itself.

MAKES: 1 filled loaf

FROM MIXING TO OVEN: 11 hours

BAKING TIME: 30–40 minutes

1. Mix the biga ingredients together, cover and leave at room temperature for 4 hours.

2. Add all the dough ingredients except the olive oil to the biga and mix together until you have an almost uniform consistency, then work in the oil until fully incorporated. Knead the dough until smooth and stretchy. It'll be sticky at first but resist the temptation to add any more flour; it's meant to be a loose dough, so just keep going until it gets silky.

3. Cover the dough and leave to rest for 5 minutes. Give the dough a double fold, cover and leave at room temperature to prove for 3 hours.

4. Give the dough another double fold to de-gas it thoroughly, cover and leave to prove for another 2½ hours.

5. Turn the dough out onto a work surface lightly dusted with flour, semolina or fine ground rice, and gently press it out into a rectangle about 20x30cm/8x12in. Smear the garlic across the dough, then lay the slices of ham side by side on top, followed by the mozzarella, tomatoes and basil.

6. Wet one short edge of the dough, then starting from the opposite edge, roll it up quite tightly like a Swiss/jelly roll, taking care that the filling stays evenly spread. Place seam-side down on a baking sheet dusted with flour, cover and leave to rise for 1 hour.

7. Heat the oven to 230°C/210°C fan/450°F/gas 8. Brush the top of the dough with olive oil, sprinkle with pepper and slash in several places through to the first layer of filling. Place in the oven on the baking sheet and bake for 20–25 minutes. Turn the heat down to 220°C/200°C fan/425°F/gas 7 and bake for a further 10–15 minutes.

FOR THE BIGA (PRE-FERMENT):

150g/5½oz/1 cup plus 2 tbsp tipo 00 bread flour

150g/5½oz/scant ⅔ cup cold water

1g/¼ tsp fresh yeast

FOR THE DOUGH:

100g/3½oz/¾ cup tipo 00 bread flour

50g/1¾oz/¼ cup durum wheat semolina (or 50g/1¾oz/6 tbsp more tipo 00 flour)

70g/2½oz/scant ⅓ cup warm water

2.5g/½ tsp fine/table salt

1g/¼ tsp fresh yeast

15g/1 tbsp olive oil

FOR THE FILLING:

1 garlic clove, crushed

30g/1oz Parma ham (or other prosciutto crudo)

150g/5½oz/about 1½ cups mozzarella, sliced very thinly

40g/1½oz/⅔ cup sundried tomatoes

1 handful fresh basil leaves

a little olive oil, for brushing

freshly ground black pepper

The Stirchley Loaf TOM BAKER

After attending "The Rise of Real Bread" conference in 2009, Tom resolved to quit his old job and match his profession to his surname. He created this loaf to celebrate helping to launch the Stirchley Community Market in 2010. Adding grated raw potato gives the bread a moister crumb, which together with the sponge and dough method prolongs its shelf life. Artificial-additive-addicted industrial loaf manufacturers take note!

MAKES: 1 large or 2 small loaves
FROM MIXING TO OVEN: overnight
plus 4–6 hours
BAKING TIME: 35–45 minutes

FOR THE SPONGE:

150g/5½oz/1 cup plus 1 tbsp white
    bread flour
150g/5½oz/scant ⅔ cup water
3g/¾ tsp fresh yeast

FOR THE DOUGH:

215g/7½oz/1 cup minus 2 tbsp water
280g/10oz/2 cups wholemeal/
    wholewheat bread flour
130g/4½oz/1 cup minus 1 tbsp white
    bread flour
65g/2¼oz/½ cup grated potato
10g/2 tsp fine/table salt

butter or oil, for greasing

1. Mix the sponge ingredients together in a bowl large enough for making 1kg/2lb 4oz of dough, cover and leave at room temperature for 8–24 hours (typically overnight) until actively bubbling.

2. For the dough, add the water to the sponge and start mixing before adding the rest of the ingredients. Continue mixing until the dough has a uniform texture, then knead the dough until it is smooth and stretchy (this will take about 10–12 minutes of active kneading, or up to 1 hour with the "fold and rest" process). Cover and leave to prove for about 3 hours until approximately doubled in volume.

3. Grease a baking sheet, shape the dough to make either 1 large loaf or 2 smaller loaves and place seam-side down on the sheet. Cover and leave to rise at room temperature for anywhere between 1 hour (summer) and 2 hours (winter).

4. Heat the oven to 230°C/210°C fan/450°F/gas 8. When the dough is fully risen, dust generously with wholemeal/wholewheat flour and slash the top with a long cut straight down the centre, or slash a pattern into the surface. Put the baking sheet with the dough on it into the oven immediately and bake for 35–45 minutes until the loaf is browned nicely and cooked through.

Tom Baker built his cob oven in 2009 and soon after founded Loaf Community Bakery and Cookery School. Inspired by meeting Dan and Johanna from The Handmade Bakery (Britain's first Community Supported Bakery), he adopted their model to sell sourdough Real Bread to neighbours. The operation moved to Stirchley town centre in 2012 with the help of a bread bond scheme. The bakery, shop and cookery school are thriving and bringing life to a down-at-heel local high street.

Carole Roberts founded LoveBread in Brighouse, West Yorkshire, in 2013. Set up as a Community Supported Bakery with a bread subscription scheme, the social enterprise also runs a volunteering scheme for people to learn new skills, and classes for local schoolchildren and community groups. Carole's bakers always use organic flour, much of it from the local Yorkshire Organic Millers, to make Real Bread by the classic British sponge and dough method.

Cheese-Topped Chilli and Onion Boule CAROLE ROBERTS

Carole told me that this bread is their signature loaf and that it is usually the first to sell out at a market, even though they make twice as much of it as any other. The recipe originally came about by accident due to someone "chucking a whole tub of chilli flakes" into her cheese and onion dough.

MAKES: 2 small loaves
FROM MIXING TO OVEN: 8–9 hours, or overnight plus 4–5 hours
BAKING TIME: 30 minutes

1. Mix the sponge ingredients together, cover and leave in the refrigerator overnight, or at room temperature for at least 4 hours.

2. Fry the onion and dried chilli/hot pepper flakes in the oil until translucent, then leave to cool before adding the sponge and the remaining dough ingredients except the cheese. Mix until you have a smooth but loose (i.e. wet and sticky) dough; don't throw in more flour. Put the dough into a bowl, cover and leave to rise for 2 hours.

3. Lightly wet the work surface, tip the dough out onto it and gently stretch it out into a 30x40cm/12x16in rectangle. You may find this easier to do in two stages, with a 10-minute rest in between.

4. Scatter half the cheese over the dough, pressing it in very lightly so it just sticks, taking care not to deflate the dough. Slightly lift the dough by its left-hand edge, folding the left-hand third to cover the middle third, then fold the right-hand third over, to cover the dough you've just folded. Turn the dough by 90 degrees and repeat this folding, then leave to rest for about 10 minutes.

5. Divide the dough into 2 equal-size pieces and shape into boules, then put into well-floured proving baskets. Cover and leave to rise for 1 hour, or until fully risen. Heat the oven to 220°C/200°C fan/425°F/ gas 7 with a large baking stone or baking sheet in place.

6. Scatter some semolina onto a peel, turn the first loaf onto it and carefully but quickly slash the top. Sprinkle on half of the remaining cheese and slide the loaf onto the baking stone. Repeat for the second loaf, using up the last of the cheese. Bake for 10 minutes, then turn the oven down to 200°C/180°C fan/400°F/gas 6 and continue to bake for another 20 minutes.

FOR THE SPONGE:
50g/1¾oz/heaping ⅓ cup white bread flour
50g/1¾oz/3½ tbsp water
a pinch of fresh yeast

FOR THE DOUGH:
1 onion, chopped finely
1 tsp dried chilli/hot pepper flakes (more or less, according to taste)
25g/2 tbsp olive oil
500g/1lb 2oz/3½ cups white bread flour
50g/1¾oz/¼ cup semolina
5g/1 tsp fresh yeast
5g/1 tsp fine/table salt
325g/11½oz/1⅓ cup water
150g/5½oz/1⅓ cups grated Cheddar cheese

Trub Trencher CHRIS YOUNG

MAKES: 2 small loaves

FROM MIXING TO OVEN: 8–13 hours

BAKING TIME: 15–20 minutes

This unusual loaf is made using trub, the yeasty sediment (or lees) found at the bottom of beer-fermenting vessels. So it's for the home brewer, or readers who know a tame brewer who will give them some trub for their starter. Try cutting the top off the trencher and using each half as a plate, or maybe just tear off chunks and enjoy with good butter, a hunk of proper cheese and a glass of the real ale it was made with.

250g/9oz/generous 1 cup trub starter

225g/8oz/scant 1 cup dark, malty beer

300g/10½oz/2 cups plus 2 tbsp wholemeal/wholewheat bread flour

200g/7oz/1½ cups minus 1 tbsp white bread flour

8g/1½ tsp fine/table salt

1. Several days before you want to bake, make the trub starter by first adding 50g/1¾oz/heaping ⅓ cup flour and 50g/1¾oz/3½ tbsp water to 50g/1¾oz/3½ tbsp of trub, and then proceeding in the same way as for the sourdough starter on page 14 until you have at least 250g/9oz/ generous 1 cup to work with.

2. When you are ready to bake, heat the beer gently in a saucepan and simmer it for a few minutes to reduce the alcohol content. If you have a suitable thermometer, check to see that it is at 80°C/175°F or higher. Remove from the heat and leave to cool.

3. Thoroughly mix the trub starter and cooled beer with the other ingredients. Cover and leave to rest for 10 minutes, then knead the dough until smooth and stretchy. Cover and leave at room temperature until doubled in size and the dough doesn't spring back instantly when gently pressed: this could take 6–10 hours. During this time, give it a single fold after the first 30, 60 and 90 minutes.

4. Divide the dough into 2 equal-size pieces and shape into balls. Cover and leave to prove until the dough doesn't spring back instantly when pressed. This may take 1–2 hours.

5. Heat the oven to 250°C/230°C fan/480°F/gas 9+, or as high as it will go, with a large baking stone or baking sheet in place. The dough should have spread during proving, making loaves that are about 25cm/10in in diameter and 3cm/1¼in high. If they aren't, you might want to gently stretch them out before baking. Using a well-floured peel, transfer the loaves onto the baking stone and turn the temperature down to 230°C/210°C fan/450°F/gas 8. Bake for 15–20 minutes until they sound hollow when tapped on the base.

Sippet: Medieval bread trenchers were typically stale pieces sliced from coarse, dense loaves. This meant they were solid enough to use as tableware and not disintegrate even soaked in gravy or sauces. Still tough after the meal, used trenchers might be given to animals or the poor, as surely only a real trencherman would eat his own . . .

Pain de Campagne ANDREW WHITLEY

Bread recipes probably evolve over time, which may be due to lard being replaced by vegetable fat, barm by baker's yeast or locally grown wheat by imported flour. It may result from salt being reduced, or simply the baker tweaking things. Since Andrew Whitley wrote *Bread Matters* in 2006, he's been modifying some recipes, and so this is the 2016 remix of his *pain de campagne*, or French-style country bread, which appeared in that book.

MAKES: 1 large or 2 small loaves
FROM MIXING TO OVEN: 9–17 hours, or overnight plus 5 hours
BAKING TIME: 50–70 minutes

1. Mix the pre-ferment ingredients together thoroughly, cover and leave in a warm place for 4 hours or in a cool place for 12 hours (typically overnight), until actively bubbling.

2. Mix the pre-ferment with the dough ingredients, then knead the dough until it is smooth and stretchy.

3. Dust a 1kg/2lb proving basket (or two 500g/1lb ones) well with rice flour or semolina. Shape the dough to fit and dip it in the rice flour, then place it seam-side up in the basket. Cover and leave to prove in a warm place for up to 5 hours until the dough has about doubled in size.

4. Heat the oven to 220°C/200°C fan/425°F/gas 7, with a baking stone or baking sheet in place.

5. Turn the dough out onto a well-floured peel and slash the top of the dough to make the pattern of your choice. Slide the dough carefully onto the baking stone and bake for 10 minutes, then turn the oven down to 200°C/180°C fan/400°F/gas 6 and continue to bake for another 40–60 minutes until you have the crust colour that you prefer.

FOR THE PRE-FERMENT:
100g/3½oz/generous ⅓ cup wheat or rye sourdough starter
60g/2oz/½ cup wholemeal/ wholewheat bread flour
65g/2¼oz/½ cup white bread flour
75g/2½oz/scant ⅓ cup water, at 35°C/95°F

FOR THE DOUGH:
200g/7oz/1½ cups minus 1 tbsp wholemeal bread flour
200g/7oz/1½ cups minus 1 tbsp white bread flour
300g/10½oz/1¼ cups water, at 35°C/95°F
8g/1½ tsp fine/table salt

rice flour or semolina for dusting

Andrew Whitley created the wood-fired, organic Village Bakery Melmerby in 1976. A visit to Russia in the early 1990s led to him becoming an advocate of genuine sourdough bread. Andrew moved on in 2002 to found Bread Matters, publishing the award-winning book of the same name in 2006. In 2008 he joined forces with the charity Sustain to launch the Real Bread Campaign and more recently published the book *Do: Sourdough*.

Baguettes PAUL MERRY

This is the Real Baguette deal, made using a pre-ferment called a poolish: equal weights of flour and water mixed with a tiny amount of yeast. Paul says, "These light and airy baguettes have so much flavour and aroma. The crisp and delicate crust contains a creamy crumb, with large, random air bubbles." For this Real Bread you need both a white bread flour with 13–14% protein and a French T55 flour (see page 28) with more like 10% protein.

MAKES: 10 small or 5 large loaves
FROM MIXING TO OVEN: overnight plus 5–6 hours
BAKING TIME: 35 minutes per batch

FOR THE POOLISH (PRE-FERMENT):
250g/9oz/1¾ cups white bread flour
250g/9oz/1 cup plus 1 tbsp water
0.5g/⅛ tsp fresh yeast, i.e. a piece barely the size of a chickpea

FOR THE DOUGH:
750g/1lb 10oz/5⅓ cups T55 flour
400–450g/14oz–1lb/1 ⅔–1¾ cups, plus 2 tbsp water, at 20–25°C/ 68–77°F
16g/½oz/3 tsp fine/table salt
7g/1½ tsp fresh yeast

1. Mix the poolish ingredients together, cover and leave at room temperature for 12–15 hours, typically overnight. It will be ready when it has doubled in size, with a myriad of bubbles on the surface (in hot weather, use 1g/¼ tsp yeast and leave to ferment in the refrigerator).

2. Add the dough ingredients to the poolish and mix thoroughly. Knead well, cover and leave to rise for about 3 hours, giving the dough a single fold halfway through that time, when it has swelled by about a third and the surface is blistered with tiny bubbles.

3. When the dough has doubled in size, divide it into 165–170g/6oz pieces for small loaves or 330–340g/11½–12oz for large ones. Shape into balls, put on a floured surface, cover and leave for 20 minutes.

4. One piece at a time, stretch the dough out gently into a rectangle, then roll it toward you as tightly as possible to make a cylinder. To build up tension on the outer surface, use the heels of your hands to push the dough away from you, as your fingers roll it toward you (fig. 1).

5. Roll the dough back and forth, moving both hands smoothly from the middle towards the ends, spreading your fingers as you go: you are aiming for a baton of even thickness with round or pointed ends (fig. 2).

6. Place this seam-side down on a floured tray or in a rucked-up couche cloth, then repeat with the remaining pieces. Cover and leave at room temperature for 45–60 minutes until the dough doesn't spring back when pressed gently. Heat the oven to 230°C/210°C fan/450°F/ gas 8, with a baking stone or baking sheet in place.

7. Slash the top of one piece of dough several times diagonally (fig. 3), holding the blade at a shallow angle to the surface, then slide it onto the baking stone using a well-floured peel. Repeat with as many pieces of dough as the stone can hold, and bake for about 35 minutes until golden, baking any remaining loaves as a second batch.

Baker's Tip: To get the classic robust, glossy crust, using steam is essential (see page 22).

Fougasse CHRIS YOUNG

Like *focaccia*, and other flatbreads found across southern and eastern Europe, this loaf – often associated with Provence – takes its name from the Latin word for "hearth", where it would once have been baked. I've kept mine plain, but you can throw in a handful of chopped pitted olives, ham, cheese or herbs, in whatever combination you fancy. You can also drizzle yours with plain or herb-infused olive oil just before and/or after they are baked.

MAKES: 2 or 3 loaves

FROM MIXING TO OVEN: overnight plus 5½–6½ hours

BAKING TIME: 10–15 minutes

1. Mix the pre-ferment ingredients together, cover and leave at room temperature for 12 hours overnight, or until bubbling vigorously.

2. Add the dough ingredients to the pre-ferment and knead ("work to an even consistency" is probably a better term, as it's so sloppy) until you have a smooth, silky, stretchy dough that is very soft but no longer sticky. You may find that this dough is easier to make using a stand mixer with a dough hook.

3. Cover the dough and give it a series of single folds after 30, 60 and 90 minutes, then leave to rise for a further 2½–3½ hours, or until it's puffed up and has huge bubbles coming to the surface.

4. Dust the work surface well with flour and using an oiled dough scraper, turn the dough out carefully, trying not to knock out too many of the bubbles you have (well, the yeast has) worked hard to make. Divide the dough into 2 or 3 equal-size pieces, gently rounding each piece into a ball (but don't go for the full shaping process described on page 21), then roll one piece out to an oval about 1.5cm/⅝in thick.

5. Using your dough scraper, cut 3 or 4 angled slots either side of the middle of the dough to make a leaf-like pattern (see photo) and open these out slightly. Repeat the rolling and cutting with the remaining dough. Cover and leave to prove for 1 hour. Meanwhile, heat the oven to 250°C/230°C fan/480°F/gas 9+, or as high as it will go, with baking stones or baking sheets in place.

6. Using a well-floured peel, slide each fougasse onto a baking stone, then immediately turn the oven down to 220°C/200°C fan/425°F/gas 7. Bake for 10–15 minutes until golden.

FOR THE PRE-FERMENT:
300g/10½oz/2 cups plus 2 tbsp white bread flour
275g/9¾oz/1 cup plus 2 tbsp water
5g/1 tsp fresh yeast

FOR THE DOUGH:
350g/12oz/2½ cups white bread flour
250g/9oz/1 cup plus 1 tbsp water
2g/scant ½ tsp fresh yeast
50g/1¾oz/3½ tbsp olive oil
5g/1 tsp fine/table salt

kalapao CHRIS YOUNG

I have happy, diesel-scented memories of eating *kalapao* for pre-sunrise breakfasts at truck stops in Laos, while waiting for a *songthaew* bus-truck to fill up with enough people to ferry me and my backpack to the next dusty town. This type of steamed bun seems to have originated in the wheat-growing regions of northern China before spreading far and wide under various names. Here's my stripped-down, back-to-basics version.

MAKES: 8 buns
FROM MIXING TO COOKING: 2 days plus 2 hours
COOKING TIME: 20–25 minutes

FOR THE SPONGE:
60g/2¼oz/scant ½ cup plain/ all-purpose flour
5g/1 tsp fresh yeast
40g/1½oz/3 tbsp water

FOR THE DOUGH:
10g/2 tsp fresh yeast
170g/6oz/scant ¾ cup milk
300g/10½oz/2¼ cups plain/ all-purpose flour
25g/1oz/2 tbsp caster/superfine sugar
3g/½ tsp fine/table salt

FOR THE FILLING:
5g/1 tsp vegetable oil, plus extra for greasing
½ white onion, finely diced
100g/3½oz/scant ½ cup minced/ ground pork
1 sweet Chinese sausage, cut into 8 pieces
4 cloud-ear mushrooms, chopped
2 spring onions/scallions, chopped
2 eggs, hard boiled and chopped into quarters
5g/1 tsp nam pla (Thai fish sauce) or soy sauce
a pinch of freshly ground black pepper

1. Mix the sponge ingredients together, cover and leave in the refrigerator overnight.

2. To make the dough, dissolve the yeast in the milk. Add the sponge and the other dough ingredients and knead until you have a smooth, stretchy ball. Cover and leave in the refrigerator overnight again.

3. Cut the dough into 8 equal-size pieces. Shape into balls, cover and leave for 20 minutes. Meanwhile, heat the oil in a pan and fry the onion until translucent, then add the minced/ground pork and stir until barely cooked without taking on any brown colour. Add the remaining filling ingredients, cover and cook over a low heat for 3–5 minutes.

4. Grease a baking sheet. Press the dough balls out into circles about 8–10cm/3¼–4in wide. Spoon the filling equally onto the middle of each piece, bring the edges of the dough together around the filling and seal each piece well, rolling it into a ball. Place on the baking sheet 5cm/2in apart. Cover and leave at room temperature for 40 minutes.

5. Line the layers of a metal or bamboo steamer with lightly oiled baking parchment pierced with holes, or use steamer papers. Arrange the buns at least 1cm/½in apart and put the steamer, with the lid on, over a pan filled with boiling water. Steam the buns over enough heat to keep the water bubbling for 15–20 minutes. Turn off the heat and leave to stand for 5 minutes. If using a metal steamer, open the lid a little to let some excess steam escape. For once, this is one to eat warm.

Sippet: *Pao* is a corruption of the Portuguese word for bread and has relatives across Asia, including *pav* in India, *bao* in Taiwan and *pan* in Japan.

Milk Bread PAUL MERRY

MAKES: 2 small loaves
FROM MIXING TO OVEN: 5–7 hours
BAKING TIME: 30–35 minutes

Paul says, "Milk loaves, once among the British craft baker's standard list of products, have their own distinct texture and flavour, with a fine pile to the crumb, and are always at home on the teatime table." A satisfactory result can be obtained by diluting the milk with water, but using milk more generously will make the loaf richer. The sponge-and-dough process, with a cool dough at the finish, gives a fine-textured bread that keeps well.

FOR THE PRE-FERMENT:

170g/6oz/scant 1¼ cups white
  bread flour
120g/4¼oz/½ cup warm water
10g/2 tsp fresh yeast
3g/½ tsp fine/table salt

FOR THE DOUGH:

400g/14oz/scant 3 cups white
  bread flour
170g/6oz/scant ¾ cup milk
35g/1¼oz/scant ¼ cup caster/
  superfine sugar (optional)
6g/1 tsp fine/table salt
35g/1¼oz/heaping 2 tbsp butter,
  diced, plus extra for greasing

1 egg, beaten, to glaze

1. Mix the pre-ferment ingredients together thoroughly. Cover and leave at room temperature for about 1 hour, or until the surface is broken by large bubbles.

2. Add the dough ingredients, except the butter, to the pre-ferment and mix well. Knead until you have a smooth dough, then work in the butter until fully combined and the dough is once again smooth, silky and soft but not sticky. Cover and leave at room temperature for 2–3 hours until the dough has doubled in size and the surface shows fine gas bubbles and has the appearance of being pock-marked.

3. Divide the dough into 2 equal-size pieces, shape into balls, cover and leave to rest for 20 minutes. Meanwhile, grease two 500g/1lb loaf tins or a flat baking sheet.

4. Reshape the dough to fit the tins, or to bake as freestanding loaves, and place in the tins or on the sheet. Cover and leave to rise for 1–2 hours, until doubled in size and the dough doesn't spring back instantly when gently pressed.

5. Heat the oven to 180–190°C/160–170°C fan/350–375°F/gas 4–5, or 200°C/180°C fan/400°F/gas 6 if you didn't use sugar. Brush the top of the loaves with beaten egg and bake for 20 minutes, turning them round after 10 minutes if they are not baking evenly. Cover the tops of the loaves with kitchen foil if they are browning too quickly, then continue to bake for a further 10–15 minutes.

Baker's Tip: Milk bread was often sold in fancy shapes or with decorative slashes. Have a look at old baking manuals – or on the internet – for ideas.

Paul Merry has been involved with Real Bread baking and masonry ovens for over 40 years. After baking in London in the 1970s, he returned to his native Australia and built his first bakery outside Melbourne. Eleven years later, he was back in the UK, working and teaching at The Village Bakery Melmerby, before setting up his own Panary baking and wood-fired oven school and consultancy in Dorset.

Orchard Loaf TONY WETHERALL

This recipe is best made in the autumn. Tony says that he created this loaf "to showcase the freshly pressed apple juice from our own organic orchards. We add just enough to increase the complexity of flavour without making the loaf sweet." If you're lucky enough to have a local farmers' market, try there for a flavoursome natural juice, in season.

MAKES: 1 large loaf
FROM MIXING TO OVEN: overnight plus 6–7 hours
BAKING TIME: 35 minutes

1. Mix the pre-ferment ingredients together in a large bowl, cover and leave at room temperature overnight.

2. To make the dough, crumble the yeast into the water and stir until dissolved. Add to the pre-ferment, stir again, then add the remaining dough ingredients except for the salt. Mix together thoroughly, then cover and leave to rest at room temperature for 10–15 minutes.

3. Add the salt and knead until it is fully incorporated and the dough is smooth. Cover and leave to prove in the refrigerator for at least 4 hours, taking the dough out around 2 hours before you plan to bake.

4. Give the dough a single fold, return it to the bowl, cover and leave at room temperature for 90 minutes.

5. Heat the oven to 250°C/230°C fan/480°F/gas 9+, or as high as it will go. Grease a 1kg/2lb loaf tin, shape the dough, place it in the tin, cover and leave to rise at room temperature for about 30 minutes.

6. Slash the top of the loaf, place it in the oven and immediately turn the oven down to 220°C/200°C fan/425°F/gas 7. Check after 10 minutes and reduce the temperature by a further 10–20°C/20–35°F if the loaf is browning too quickly, which can happen because of the sugar in the apple juice, and bake for a further 25 minutes.

FOR THE PRE-FERMENT:
150g/5½oz/about 1 cup wholemeal/wholewheat bread flour
5g/1 tsp fresh yeast
160g/5¾oz/⅔ cup water

FOR THE DOUGH:
10g/2 tsp fresh yeast
190g/6¾oz/¾ cup plus 2 tsp warm water
300g/10½oz/2 cups plus 2 tbsp white bread flour
50g/1¾oz/3½ tbsp freshly pressed apple juice
50g/1¾oz/heaping ⅓ cup wholemeal/wholewheat bread flour
50g/1¾oz/heaping ⅓ cup wholemeal/wholegrain (dark) rye flour
15g/2 tbsp sunflower seeds
10g/1 tbsp linseeds/flaxseeds
8g/1½ tsp fine/table salt

butter or oil, for greasing

Tony Wetherall changed career in 2010 to start the Roots Bakehouse, in the shop on Will and Meg Edmonds' family farm in Worcestershire. An area was converted into a microbakery with a window onto the shop allowing customers to see the baking in action. He bakes Real Bread on Thursday and Friday and uses a wood-fired oven to run Friday-evening pizza nights.

Dineke van den Bogerd was born in Friesland and set up the Crumbs of Capel microbakery in Surrey in late 2009. At present she bakes in her small home kitchen, which limits her to making about 45 loaves a day, but she's hoping to convert a garage so she can bake more Real Bread for local people.

Fryske Sûkerbôle DINEKE VAN DEN BOGERD

Sugar, spice and all things nice? Traditionally, this loaf from the northern Netherlands would be a gift to the mother of a newborn baby girl. Because of the amount of sugar, it is a sweet, sticky, chewy occasional treat, rather than an everyday staple, especially if served as Dineke suggests, with a generous layer of butter. She says, "With all the sugar, this bread should keep for a few days, but somehow we have never been able to put that to the test."

MAKES: 2 small loaves

FROM MIXING TO OVEN: 7–8 hours, or overnight plus 4–5 hours

BAKING TIME: 30–40 minutes

1. Bring the milk to the boil, then leave to cool until hand warm. Stir in the ginger syrup and yeast until dissolved, then whisk in the flour. Cover and leave at room temperature for 2 hours.

2. Whisk the egg into the pre-ferment, then mix in the flour, ginger, cinnamon and salt. Knead the dough until smooth and stretchy.

3. Cover and leave to rise at room temperature for about 2 hours, or in the refrigerator overnight. If kept in the refrigerator, remove about 2 hours before you plan to bake and leave to return to room temperature.

4. Line two 500g/1lb loaf tins with kitchen foil, pressed flat against the sides while making sure not to tear any holes, and leaving about a 5cm/2in overlap all the way around. Grease generously with butter, and dot with about a third of the sugar, shaken around so that it sticks to all the sides.

5. Dust the work surface with flour and divide the dough into 2 equal-size pieces. Dust the tops well with flour and roll each piece out into a rectangle a little shorter than the longer side of the loaf tin and about 30cm/12in long. Holding back a little sugar for the tops, sprinkle the remainder evenly over the 2 pieces of dough, then roll each piece up tightly and place seam-side down in the loaf tins and press down gently into the corners.

6. Cover and leave to prove for about 2 hours, until the dough rises just above the tops of the tins. Heat the oven to 180°C/160°C fan/350°F/gas 4.

7. Brush each loaf with a little water and sprinkle with the remaining sugar. Bake the loaves for about 30–40 minutes until golden brown, checking that they do not burn. Remove the tins from the oven, fold the foil over the top of the loaves, remove from the tins and leave to cool in the foil.

FOR THE PRE-FERMENT:

450g/1lb/2 cups minus 2 tbsp milk

45g/1½oz/3 tbsp ginger syrup (from the stem/preserved ginger jar)

10g/2 tsp fresh yeast

350g/12oz/2½ cups white bread flour

FOR THE DOUGH:

1 egg

350g/12oz/2½ cups white bread flour

50g/1¾oz/⅓ cup stem/preserved ginger, diced

5g/1 tsp ground cinnamon

8g/1½ tsp fine/table salt

butter, for greasing

450g/1lb/2¼ cups pearl (nibbed) sugar, or sugar cubes each roughly crushed into about 8 pieces

Gaye Whitwam runs a microbakery at her home in the Surrey suburbs of Greater London. As well as baking for a local farmers' market, she is a leading figure in the Bread Angels network, teaching other people to make Real Bread and set up their own microbakeries.

Saffron Cake GAYE WHITWAM

Gaye was born in Cornwall just after the Second World War. She told me "this bread evokes everything that was good about my childhood. Everything that was not so good is best forgotten and compensated for by a piece of toasted saffron cake with Cornish butter, naturally, and a good cup of English tea."

MAKES: 1 loaf
FROM MIXING TO OVEN: 9–12 hours
BAKING TIME: 50 minutes

1. Heat the milk, dried fruit, saffron and lemon zest in a pan until barely boiling, simmer briefly, then leave to cool for 15–20 minutes.

2. Strain the milk into a bowl, reserving the fruit separately. Measure the milk and make up to 160g/5¾oz/⅔ cup.

3. Rub the yeast into the wholemeal/wholewheat flour, then stir in the milk. Cover and leave at room temperature for about 1 hour, or until the mixture has puffed up and there are bubbles on the surface.

4. Add the white flour, sugar and salt and mix thoroughly. If the dough won't come together into a consistent mass, add a few more drops of milk. Knead until you have a smooth dough, then cover and leave it to rest for 10 minutes.

5. Knead the butter and reserved fruit into the dough, working it until it comes together again. Continue kneading until the dough is smooth and stretchy, then return it to the bowl, cover and leave to prove in the refrigerator for 6–8 hours until it looks puffy again. Remove from the refrigerator about 1 hour before you plan to bake.

6. Grease a 1kg/2lb loaf tin. Turn the dough out onto a lightly floured work surface, pressing it into a rectangle slightly shorter than the long side of the loaf tin. Roll the dough up into a log, then place it seam-side down in the tin. Cover and leave to rise for about 40 minutes.

7. Heat the oven to 200°C/180°C fan/400°F/gas 6. Brush the top of the dough with beaten egg and bake for 10 minutes, then turn the oven down to 180°C/160°C fan/350°F/gas 4 and continue to bake for a further 40 minutes, checking halfway through and covering loosely with kitchen foil if it is browning too quickly. Turn the loaf out of the tin and leave to cool on a wire rack.

160g/5¾oz/⅔ cup milk, plus a little extra
100g/3½oz/¾ cup mixed dried fruit
0.2g/a good pinch of saffron strands
zest of 1 unwaxed lemon
5g/1 tsp fresh yeast
200g/7oz/1½ cups minus 1 tbsp wholemeal/wholewheat bread flour
200g/7oz/1½ cups minus 1 tbsp white bread flour
70g/2½oz/⅓ cup packed light soft brown sugar
2g/½ tsp fine/table salt
65g/2¼oz/¼ cup butter, softened, plus extra for greasing
1 egg, beaten, to glaze

Christmas Bread ANDREW WHITLEY

MAKES: 1 large or 2 small loaves

FROM MIXING TO OVEN: overnight plus 4½–6½ hours

BAKING TIME: 30–60 minutes, depending on loaf size

While other nations have their *stollen* and *panettone*, when it comes to Christmas, here in Britain we tend to put our dried fruits and spices into cakes, puddings and mince pies. However, in *English Bread and Yeast Cookery*, Elizabeth David mentioned a Christmas bread recipe from Cumbria, which inspired Andrew to write this modern version. Yeast has a hard time when dough is enriched with butter and sugar, and using a pre-ferment helps get that "rise".

FOR THE PRE-FERMENT:

175g/6oz/1¼ cups white bread flour

5g/1 tsp fresh yeast

125g/4½oz/½ cup water, at about 25°C/75°F

FOR THE FRUIT AND NUT SOAKER:

100g/3½oz/½ cup crystallized/ candied ginger, chopped

100g/3½oz/¾ cup raisins or sultanas/ golden raisins

100g/3½oz/1 cup dried cranberries

50g/1¾oz/⅓ cup pitted dates, chopped

50g/1¾oz/⅓ cup dried figs, quartered

100g/3½oz/scant 1 cup almonds or Brazil nuts, chopped

50g/1¾oz/3⅓ tbsp rum, brandy or fruit juice

FOR THE DOUGH:

220g/7¾oz/1½ cups white bread flour

100g/3½oz/7 tbsp butter, plus extra for greasing

70g/2½oz/⅓ cup packed dark brown sugar

100g/3½oz lightly beaten egg, (about 2 eggs)

1. Mix the pre-ferment ingredients together thoroughly, cover and leave in the refrigerator for about 12 hours overnight. Meanwhile, mix the soaker ingredients together in a bowl, substituting similar fruits, nuts and liquid if you wish, according to taste, allergies or simply what you have to hand. Leave this mixture at room temperature for about 12 hours, stirring occasionally.

2. Mix the dough ingredients into the pre-ferment and knead until the sticky mixture becomes a soft, smooth and glossy dough. Cover and leave at room temperature for 2–3 hours. At this point you can give it a fold and leave it for another hour or so, but this isn't essential.

3. Tip the dough out onto a lightly floured work surface and pat it into a rectangle about 20x25cm/8x10in. Spread the fruit and nut soaker over almost all the surface. Roll the dough up carefully, turn it through 90 degrees and gently roll it up again, taking care not to force the fruit through the surface. The aim is even distribution, but it is better to leave the dough a bit lumpy than to work it so much that you end up with a mess.

4. Grease the baking tin (or tins) with butter, shape the dough to fit and place it in the tin(s). Cover and leave to rise at room temperature for about 2 hours, or until the dough doesn't spring back instantly when gently pressed. Heat the oven to 180°C/160°C fan/350°F/gas 4.

5. Bake a large loaf for 45–60 minutes, smaller ones for about 30–40 minutes, until the top is a deep golden brown.

Baker's Tip: For an extra glossy crust, you can brush the top of the dough with a little beaten egg before baking or with melted butter afterward. For a festive flourish, dust the top with icing/confectioners' sugar when it has cooled.

Long Ferment

As demonstrated by many industrial bakers, a loaf of sorts can be made in under a couple of hours from start to finish. The thing is, like certain other things in life, does a quick finish necessarily give the most satisfaction?

Even when you're not using a sourdough starter, lowering the proving temperature and reducing the amount of yeast will mean the dough takes longer to be ready. As with other methods in this book, this extra time allows all sorts of bready alchemy to go on, turning even relatively unremarkable ingredients into what you might agree is a far superior loaf to one that's been banged out as fast as possible.

Cottage Loaf SONYA HUNDAL

By 1977, Elizabeth David might have waxed nostalgic about the cottage loaf, but still within the context of bakeries making it. It graced the cover of that year's Ladybird bread book for children, and of *The Sunday Times Book of Real Bread* in 1982. Today? I can't remember the last time I saw one outside a baking competition. Sonya's recipe is unusual in adding dashes of wholemeal/wholewheat and rye flours to the usual white.

MAKES: 1 very large loaf
FROM MIXING TO OVEN: 5–6 hours
BAKING TIME: 30–45 minutes

625g/1lb 6oz/4½ cups white bread flour

40g/1½oz/scant ⅓ cup wholemeal/wholewheat bread flour

25g/1oz/scant ¼ cup wholemeal/wholegrain (dark) rye flour

10g/2 tsp fresh yeast (reduce to 4g/scant 1 tsp if room temperature is above 20°C/68°F)

9g/1¾ tsp fine/table salt

450g/1lb/2 cups minus 2 tbsp water at 18–20°C/65–68°F

1. Stir all the flours together, then rub the yeast into the flour. Add the salt and most of the water and mix together thoroughly, then knead the dough for 10 minutes. This needs to be a stiff dough but if it's so stiff that you can't knead it, or any dry patches remain, gradually add more of the water. Cover and leave to rise at a cool room temperature (15–18°C/60–65°F) for 2 hours, then give the dough a single fold, cover again, and leave to rise for another 45–60 minutes.

2. Tip the dough out onto a lightly floured work surface. The side of the dough in contact with the floured surface is the "good side" and will end up as the top of the loaf. Shape the dough into a ball, return to the bowl good side down, cover and leave to rise for 1 hour.

3. Divide the dough into 2 pieces, one about half the size of the other (so the smaller piece weighs about 360–370g/12¾–13oz), then flatten each piece to thoroughly de-gas the dough and shape each piece tightly into a ball, to keep a defined shape for baking. Cover the dough and leave for a final 45–60 minute rise. Meanwhile, heat the oven to 220°C/200°C fan/425°F/gas 7, with a baking stone or baking sheet in place, leaving sufficient headspace for your loaf.

4. Slightly flatten each ball and place the smaller on top of the larger one. Using a thumb and two fingers pinched together, or a wooden spoon handle (some old-school bakers used an elbow), push a deep dimple straight down through the middle of the top ball and well into the lower one. With a really stiff dough, you can go down to the work surface. Cover and leave the dough to rest for 10 minutes.

5. If you like, you can snip or slash vertical notches on one or both parts of the loaf just before it goes into the oven. Using a floured peel, lift the dough onto the baking stone and bake for 10–15 minutes, then turn the oven down to 180°C/160°C fan/350°F/gas 4 and continue to bake for a further 20–30 minutes until well browned.

Sonya Hundal is a writer and baker who set up Greenfield Bakers in 2008 in a converted stable in Friskney, on the coastal strip of rural Lincolnshire. She bakes slow-fermentation breads all made from stoneground organic flour from the Maud Foster Windmill in Boston, some with added locally seasonal ingredients. They are baked directly on the floor of her wood-fired clay oven "by a contented human being".

Remek Sanetra learnt his baking skills in the UK over 20 years ago but his passion started back home in Poland. There, under the communist regime, he has childhood memories of queuing on Saturdays for good bread that lasted a week. With an air that some of his colleagues liken at times to a "mad professor", Remek carefully nurtures each of The Flour Station's starters to deliver Real Bread across London every day.

Wholemeal Dark Rye and Potato Bread REMEK SANETRA

This reminds me of a pumpernickel, though traditionally that would have a much longer sourdough fermentation and long, slow baking in covered tins. But don't bake the potatoes for this recipe on their own: save energy and cook something else at the same time, such as another loaf, or tonight's dinner.

MAKES: 1 loaf
FROM MIXING TO OVEN: 1 day
  plus 6–7 hours
BAKING TIME: 55 minutes

1. Cover the chopped rye grains with the water and leave to soak for 24 hours.

2. Heat the oven to 220°C/200°C fan/425°F/gas 7. Bake the potato for 1 hour or until soft, then leave to cool. Scrape the flesh out of the skin, mash it and weigh 235g/8½oz/1 cup of it to use in the dough.

3. Mix the rye soaker, mashed potato and all of the other ingredients together thoroughly, working the dough for a few minutes until it changes from brown to a lighter, yellower shade. Because of the low gluten content, you can't knead it in the same way as a wheat dough, and it will be very wet and sticky. Cover the dough and leave at room temperature for about 3 hours until it has puffed up and is starting to show little holes on the surface.

4. Grease a 1kg/2lb loaf tin. Dust the work surface with rye flour and turn the dough out onto it. Shape the dough to fit, place it in the tin, flatten the top with wetted fingers and dust the top with rye flour. Cover and leave at room temperature for 1–2 hours, or until you see cracks appearing on the surface of the dough.

5. Heat the oven to 240°C/220°C fan/475°F/gas 8–9. Dust the top of the dough again with rye flour, put it into the oven and bake for 20 minutes, then turn the oven down to 190°C/170°C fan/375°F/gas 5 and bake for a further 35 minutes, or until the loaf has a rich dark crust.

FOR THE SOAKER:

55g/2oz/⅓ cup chopped rye grains

60g/2¼oz/¼ cup cold water

FOR THE DOUGH:

1 or 2 large baking potatoes (a floury/
  starchy, rather than waxy, variety)

60g/2¼oz/¼ cup rye sourdough
  starter (see page 14)

200g/7oz/¾ cup plus 1 tbsp water

235g/8½oz/heaping 2 cups
  wholemeal/wholegrain (dark)
  rye flour

10g/2 tsp fresh yeast

8g/1½ tsp fine/table salt

190g/6¾oz/1⅓ cups sunflower seeds

45g/1½oz/2 tbsp black treacle/
  molasses

butter or oil, for greasing

Baker's Tip: This bread positively improves with age and is best enjoyed the day after baking.

Overnight White SID PRICE

This recipe has stayed almost the same since Sid Price made it in 1943. Deborah Cook, Sid's granddaughter says, "We've always made Real Bread! The only change, apart from converting from Imperial to metric measurements, is that we've reduced the salt level slightly." Fermenting dough slowly overnight with a very small amount of yeast allows time to develop maximum flavour, a great crust and a loaf that will keep longer.

MAKES: 1 large loaf

FROM MIXING TO OVEN: overnight plus 2½ hours

BAKING TIME: 45 minutes

500g/1lb 2oz/3½ cups white bread flour

8g/1½ tsp fine/table salt

2g/½ tsp lard

1.5g/¼ tsp fresh yeast

280g/10oz/1¼ cups minus 1 tbsp water

butter or oil, for greasing

1. Mix all of the ingredients together thoroughly, then knead quite firmly until you have a smooth and stretchy dough. As it is so tight (which means the ratio of water to flour is quite low), you might need to stop and leave the dough to rest for 10 minutes before continuing. Cover and leave to rise at room temperature overnight.

2. Grease a large loaf tin, shape the dough to fit and place it in the tin. Cover and leave to prove at room temperature for 2 hours.

3. Heat the oven to 240–250°C/220–230°C fan/475–500°F/gas 8–9, or as high as it will go. Dust the top of the dough with flour, if you like, slash down the middle of the loaf and bake for 45 minutes.

Sid Price bought the bakery on Castle Street in Ludlow, Shropshire, in 1943. He ran the bakehouse and shop with his wife and the help of several of their 12 children, amazingly finding time to serve three terms as the town's mayor. After Sid passed away in 1977, the business was inherited by three of his children, of whom Sheila is still a co-owner with two of her daughters.

Plain Maslin Loaf CHRIS YOUNG

In an age where cereal monoculture is the norm, it might come as a surprise to learn that fields once swayed with not only different varieties of the same grain, but also mixes of different cereals. At one time it was not unusual to have wheat and rye grown, harvested and milled together. Other grains might also find themselves in the mix. The resulting meal, and bread made from it, was known as maslin, which was my inspiration for this lovable mongrel of a loaf.

MAKES: 1 large loaf
FROM MIXING TO OVEN: 5½–8 hours
BAKING TIME: 40–50 minutes

300g/10½oz/2 cups plus 2 tbsp wholemeal/wholegrain bread flour
150g/5½oz/1 cup white bread flour
100g/3½oz/¾ cup wholemeal (dark) rye flour
50g/1¾oz/½ cup rolled oats
400g/14oz/1 ⅔ cups water
5g/1 tsp fresh yeast
8g/1½ tsp fine/table salt
butter or oil, for greasing

1. Mix all of the ingredients except the butter together thoroughly and then knead until you have a smooth and stretchy dough. Cover and leave to rise at room temperature for about 4 hours – if the room is cooler, it could take up to 6 hours. At this point, you can go shopping, watch TV, set off on a bracing walk or whatever; the dough won't have abandonment issues.

2. Turn the dough out onto a floured work surface and gently press to deflate it a little and form it into a square-ish shape. If baking a sandwich loaf, roll the dough up like a Swiss/jelly roll and place it seam-side down in a greased large loaf tin. Alternatively, shape into a cob (round) loaf by pulling the corners into the middle of the dough and pressing down, repeating with the four new corners you've made, then flipping this over, tucking-in and smoothing any sticking-out bits with your hands and placing on a greased baking sheet. Cover and leave to rise again for 1½–2 hours.

3. Heat the oven to 230°C/210°C fan/450°F/gas 8. Bake the loaf for 10 minutes, then turn the oven down to 200°C/180°C/400°F/gas 6 and bake for a further 30–40 minutes. Remove the loaf from the tin or baking sheet and leave on a wire cooling rack until cold.

Sippet: The word maslin is assumed to come from the Latin for mixed, via Old French and Middle English.

No-knead White Loaf

KELLIANNE DI CAPRI

As this is a fairly high hydration (wet) dough, it gets a long baking, which also gives a darker-coloured loaf. Uncooked bread dough has none of the charms of cookie dough, and I don't see any ice-cream makers turning it into a popular flavour in the foreseeable future, so sometimes it is better to opt for a little more time in the oven.

MAKES: 1 loaf
FROM MIXING TO OVEN: 10 hours, or overnight plus 2 hours
BAKING TIME: 50–60 minutes

1. Crumble the yeast into the water in a large bowl and stir until dissolved, then add the flour and salt and mix everything together thoroughly. You will have a very loose, wet and shaggy dough.

2. Cover the bowl and leave to rise in the refrigerator for at least 8 hours or overnight.

3. Grease a 1kg/2lb loaf tin well and dust the inside with plenty of flour.

4. Take the bowl of dough from the refrigerator, deflate the dough gently and, with wet hands and dough scrapers, remove all the dough from the bowl.

5. Keeping your hands wet and using swift but careful movements to avoid the dough sticking to your hands, try to shape it to fit the loaf tin. Place it in the tin, seam-side down.

6. Dust the top of the loaf well with flour, cover and leave to rise at room temperature for about 2 hours.

7. Heat the oven to 200°C/180°C fan/400°F/gas 6. Bake the loaf for 50–60 minutes until really well browned.

7g/1½ tsp fresh yeast
375g/13oz/1½ cups plus 1 tbsp warm water
500g/1lb 2oz/3½ cups white bread flour
7g/1½ tsp fine/table salt
butter, for greasing

Kellianne Di Capri trained as a boulanger in Paris and has worked as a baker in one way or another for the past 15 years. She set up her home-based microbakery and baking school in Llandinam, Powys, Wales, in 2013. She says, "I am a total breadhead and an utterly unrepentant Real Bread obsessive. I truly believe that if people ate more Real Bread, we would be happier . . . probably."

Rustic Lincolnshire Poacher and Onion Bread SONYA HUNDAL

Sonya's bakery is about 50 miles/80km from where Lincolnshire Poacher cheese is made. She says it "has a distinctive nutty flavour when cooked and is nicely balanced with the sweet flavour from the onions". Do substitute a different hard, mature/sharp cheese if you can't get this one, but you'll have to give the loaf a different name.

MAKES: 1 large loaf or 2 small loaves
FROM MIXING TO OVEN: 5–6 hours
BAKING TIME: 25–45 minutes

1. Whisk the yeast into the water until dissolved, then add the 3 different flours with the salt and mix thoroughly. Cover and leave at a cool room temperature (ideally 15–18°C/60–65°F) for 2 hours.

2. Give the dough a single fold, cover and leave for a further 45–60 minutes until the dough has noticeably increased in size; you may notice an aroma similar to ripe bananas.

3. Tip the dough out onto a lightly floured work surface. The side of the dough in contact with the floured surface is the "good" side and will end up as the top of the loaf. You can divide the dough into 2 equal-size pieces at this point, if you would prefer 2 small loaves.

4. Gently round the dough into a boule without using the full shaping process on page 21, ending with it "good" side down on a floured surface. Cover and leave to prove for 1 hour.

5. Flatten the dough down gently and place the onion and cheese in the middle. Fold the nearest and furthest edges over the middle so they overlap, pressing down with your fingers to seal in the onion and cheese.

6. Fold the left and right ends of the dough in to form points, then fold these almost to the middle of the dough, pressing them down to seal. Roll the dough backwards and forwards 2 or 3 times, ending with the "good" side facing up. Do any tucking-in needed at the bottom to create a neat oval shape, cover and leave to prove for 1–1½ hours.

7. Heat the oven to 250°C/230°C fan/480°F/gas 9+, or as high as it will go, with a baking stone or baking sheet in place. Make 3 slashes in the dough and dust with flour, then slide it onto the baking stone using a floured peel. Bake for 15 minutes, then turn the oven down to 220°C/200°C fan/425°F/gas 7 and continue to bake for another 25–30 minutes (large loaf) or 10–15 minutes (small loaves).

10g/2 tsp fresh yeast (reduce to 6g/1¼ tsp if room temperature is much above 20°C/68°F)

400g/14oz/1⅔ cups water, at about 20°C/68°F

600g/1lb 5oz/4¼ cups white bread flour

40g/1½oz4½ tbsp wholemeal/ wholewheat bread flour

30g/1oz/4 tbsp wholemeal/wholegrain (dark) rye flour

10g/2 tsp fine/table salt

60g/2¼oz/½ cup diced onion

60g/2¼oz/⅔ cup Lincolnshire Poacher cheese, coarsely grated

Sippet: Lincolnshire Poacher is a hard, unpasteurized cow's milk cheese, made by a process that is similar to traditional Cheddar, and matured for up to 24 months.

Dragan Bread DRAGAN MATIJEVIC

This loaf is the creation of "Magic" Dragan, the Conjuring Croatian. He says, "The smell of the loaves baking is enough to lift the spirits on even the dullest day!", and that blend of honey, fruit, nuts and spices is guaranteed to lift your spirits. It goes well with cheese and I'm assured it makes outstanding toast for breakfast, if there's any left by then.

MAKES: 2 small loaves
FROM MIXING TO OVEN: 6 hours
BAKING TIME: 35 minutes

500g/1lb 2oz/3½ cups white bread flour
150g/5½oz/⅔ cup white sourdough starter
350g/12oz/1½ cups water
30g/1oz/about 2 tbsp honey
3g/¾ tsp fresh yeast
10g/2 tsp fine/table salt
5 cardamom pods
200g/7oz/1½ cups pitted prunes, chopped
150g/5½oz/1½ cups walnuts, quartered
2–3 tsp ground cumin

1. Mix the flour, sourdough starter, water, honey and yeast together thoroughly. Cover and leave at room temperature for 1 hour.

2. Stretch the dough out, scatter the salt over it and then knead until you have a smooth, stretchy dough. Cover the dough and leave to relax for 10 minutes.

3. Crush the seeds from the cardamom pods in a mortar and pestle, discarding the husks. Flatten out the dough and spread evenly with the prunes, walnuts, cumin and cardamom. Knead until all the ingredients are incorporated and evenly distributed, then shape the dough into a ball. Cover and leave for 30 minutes before giving the dough a single fold.

4. Leave for a further 30 minutes before giving the dough another single fold, then cover and leave to rise for a further 2 hours.

5. Divide the dough into 2 equal-size pieces, shape into balls, cover and leave to rest for 15 minutes.

6. Dust two 500g/1lb proving baskets with flour. Shape the dough balls to fit and place them seam-side up in the baskets. Cover and leave to rise at room temperature for 1 hour.

7. Heat the oven to 230°C/210°C fan/450°F/gas 8, with a large baking stone or baking sheet in place. Turn the loaves out onto a floured peel. Slash the top of each loaf, slide them gently onto the baking stone and bake for 35 minutes.

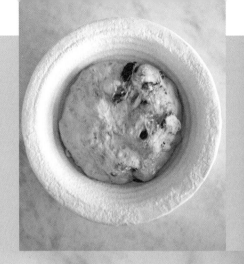

Dragan Matijevic started baking when he arrived in the UK from what was Yugoslavia in the 1970s and was shocked by what was sold as "bread". He and his partner Penny later created what they called "the world's smallest bakery" at home. In 2013, they moved to the edge of Dartmoor National Park and set up the Artisan Bakery School, teaching people both baking and business skills to launch their own microbakeries or micropizzerias.

Scott Hayward was born in London and worked as a chef for many years. When offered the chance to become a baker at Olivia's Bakery & Café in Darlington, he dived right in and took over as head baker in 2011. Olivia's is a social enterprise that offers training placements to disadvantaged young people, helping them to improve their self-confidence and contribute positively to their local community. Scott now runs the wholesale part of the business, promoting Real Bread to the region's finest restaurants and hotels.

Stout, Stilton and Walnut Bread

SCOTT HAYWARD

Historically, stout was a type of porter: a dark beer, made from well-roasted barley, and with a higher alcohol content. Today, though the colour remains the same, it's usually lower in alcohol, but this makes it an ideal, flavoursome alternative to water when bread making, particularly when teamed with other sophisticated flavours.

MAKES: 2 small loaves

FROM MIXING TO OVEN: 4–5 hours

BAKING TIME: 30–40 minutes

1. Mix the stout and yeast together until dissolved, then add the other ingredients, except the walnuts and cheese, and mix thoroughly.

2. Knead the dough until smooth and stretchy, cover and leave to relax at room temperature for 10 minutes.

3. Press the dough out gently to form a rectangle, scatter the cheese and nuts over it, roll the dough up and knead until mixed in, trying not to mash the cheese up too much. Cover the dough and leave to prove at room temperature for 3 hours.

4. Divide the dough into 2 equal-size pieces and shape into balls. Cover and leave to relax for 10 minutes.

5. Reshape the balls, dust with flour, cover and leave to prove at room temperature for 1 hour, either seam-side down on a floured work surface or seam-side up in floured proving baskets.

6. Heat the oven to 220°C/200°C fan/425°F/gas 7, with a large baking stone or baking sheet in place. Transfer the loaves to a floured peel, seam-side down. Slash the top of each loaf, then slide them gently onto the baking stone. Bake for 30–40 minutes until golden brown.

350g/12oz/1½ cups stout or porter

5g/1 tsp fresh yeast

365g/12¾oz/2½ cups plus 1 tbsp white bread flour

305g/10¾oz/2 cups plus 2 tbsp wholemeal/wholewheat bread flour

10g/2 tsp fine/table salt

10g/1 tsp black treacle/molasses

75g/2½oz/¾ cup walnuts, toasted and chopped

75g/2½oz/¾ cup Stilton cheese, cut into 1cm/½in cubes

Sippet: Stilton is a blue-veined cheese made in the English counties of Nottinghamshire, Derbyshire or Leicestershire. Due to its legally protected status, it cannot be made in the Cambridgeshire village which gave it its name.

Baker's Tip: As this is a Real Bread book, you won't be surprised if I suggest the stout you use is a real ale with complexity and depth of flavour, rather than some bland mass-produced fizz.

Einkorn Bread CLARE MARRIAGE

Einkorn (*Triticum monococcum*) is one of man's earliest crops, with evidence of cultivation from at least 8000BC. While not suitable for a wheat- or gluten-free diet, some people who have trouble with modern wheat varieties may find it more digestible. Clare says, "Einkorn flour may absorb more liquid than other flours and can become sticky with excessive kneading." Her recipe makes a characterful dark loaf, with an even crumb and good flavour.

MAKES: 1 large loaf
FROM MIXING TO OVEN: 10–15 hours, or overnight
BAKING TIME: 1 hour

5g/1 tsp fresh yeast
500g/1lb 2oz/scant 4¼ cups wholemeal/wholegrain einkorn flour
400g/14oz/1⅔ cups water
5g/1 tsp fine/table salt
butter, for greasing

1. Rub the yeast into the flour, add the water and salt and mix thoroughly.

2. Cover the bowl and leave at room temperature for 10–15 hours, or overnight if that suits you.

3. Heat the oven to 240°C/220°C fan/475°F/gas 8–9. Grease a 1kg/2lb loaf tin and a sheet of kitchen foil which will be used to cover the bread as it bakes (or use a Pullman loaf tin, greasing the inside, including inside the lid).

4. With a wetted dough scraper, scoop the dough into the tin and cover with the foil, leaving enough space for the dough to rise in the oven. Leave to rest for 10 minutes.

5. Bake the loaf for 30 minutes, then remove the foil and turn the oven down to 200°C/180°C fan/400°F/gas 6. Continue to bake for a further 30 minutes.

Clare Marriage and her husband Michael converted the family's Doves Farm to organic agriculture in 1978, establishing a business that continues to thrive. They remain active members of both the organic and Slow Food movements.

ciabatta STEVE NATHAN

The name comes from the Italian word for slipper, perhaps because of the similarity in shape. Some might argue that many industrial versions of this bread also have the taste and texture of footwear! This recipe uses a very wet dough, which allows the gluten to stretch to its limits, creating a very open network of large holes in the crumb. Please don't be scared of how wet it is, or be tempted to throw in extra flour.

MAKES: 2 large loaves

FROM MIXING TO OVEN: 4–5 hours

BAKING TIME: 20–30 minutes

1. Mix the flour and water together thoroughly in a large bowl. Cover and leave for 20–60 minutes, then tip the dough onto the work surface and sprinkle with the salt and yeast. Knead until it is smooth, shiny and starts to resist further kneading, then return the dough to the bowl, cover and leave at room temperature for 40 minutes.

2. Pat the dough out into a rectangle on the work surface, then fold the left-hand third of the dough over the middle third, and the right-hand third over the dough you've just folded. Return the dough to the bowl for 40 minutes, then turn it out again and give it a double fold: in from left and right, then fold the edge furthest from you over the middle, finally folding the edge nearest you over the "parcel" of dough. Return it to the bowl, seam-side down, and leave for another 40 minutes.

3. Place the dough on a well-floured work surface, seam-side down. Flour your hands and swiftly stretch the dough into a rectangle about 2cm/¾in thick. Cut this halfway along its length, to form 2 loaves and dust well with flour. Cover loosely and leave to rise at room temperature for 90 minutes until the dough feels light and puffy.

4. Heat the oven to 250°C/230°C fan/480°F/gas 9+, with a baking stone or baking sheet in place. Lift each ciabatta in turn, sliding your fingers under the short ends of the dough and bringing them slightly closer together as you do so, then carefully lower the dough onto the hot baking stone, giving it a slight stretch as you do to form the characteristic "dog-bone" shape. Bake for 20–30 minutes until the loaves are golden and crispy on the outside.

500g/1lb 2oz/3½ cups white bread flour
375g/13oz/1½ cups plus 1 tbsp water
8g/1½ tsp fine/table salt
10g/2 tsp fresh yeast, finely crumbled

Steve Nathan is a self-taught baker, who says he has developed his skills over more than a decade of "elaborate and messy trial and error". He teaches classes at Eastcourt Manor in Kent, which dates back to the early 14th century.

Baker's Tip: If you have an industrial-strength food mixer with a dough hook, this is one to use it for.

Naan ANDREW SMITH

MAKES: 2 naan

FROM MIXING TO OVEN: overnight plus
1½ hours

BAKING TIME: 1–2 minutes in a tandoor;
12–15 minutes in a domestic oven

From the small ones used to mop up prawn/shrimp korma at The Bengal or Raj Duth in Lichfield to the family-size versions found in Birmingham's Balti Triangle, I have only happy memories of pillowy naan breads. Without a tandoor oven to give your dough a short, sharp burst of heat on both sides, it's hard to perfect. But then I thought some people reading this book might have pizza ovens, or simply fancy giving it a go.

500g/1lb 2oz/3½ cups white bread
  flour
200g/7oz/¾ cup plus 1 tbsp water,
  at 19°C/66°F
125g/4½oz/½ cup plain live yogurt
50g/1¾oz beaten egg (about 1 egg)
25g/1oz/⅓ cup milk powder
8g/1½ tsp fresh yeast
8g/1½ tsp fine/table salt
4g/¾ tsp vegetable oil
melted butter or ghee, for brushing

1. Mix all of the ingredients together thoroughly. Cover and leave to rest at room temperature for 10 minutes.

2. Knead the dough until smooth and stretchy. Cover and leave to prove in the refrigerator overnight.

3. Divide the dough into 2 equal-size pieces and stretch them out to teardrop or circular shapes about 1cm/½in thick. Cover and leave to rise on a well-floured surface at room temperature for about 1 hour.

4. Heat your tandoor or pizza oven to 400–500°C/750–930°F, or crank your domestic oven up as high as it will go, with a baking stone in place. With your hand well protected from the heat, slap each piece of dough onto the inside wall of the tandoor (if you have one, you'll know how to use it better and more safely than I can advise you), or use a well-floured peel to slide it onto the hot baking stone. Bake for about 90 seconds in a tandoor or pizza oven, or without steam for 12–15 minutes in a domestic oven.

5. Brush the top of each naan generously with melted butter and serve as soon as possible with your favourite curry or stew.

Andrew Smith was a founder member of the Red Herring Workers' Co-operative in Newcastle upon Tyne; a bakery supervisor at The Village Bakery Melmerby; bakery lecturer at Leeds City College, Newcastle College and Gateshead College; and has assisted on Bread Matters' courses. As founder of Bread and Roses in Alnwick, Northumberland, he continues to bake Real Bread professionally, as well as offer training and consultancy.

Simit CHRIS YOUNG

Having spent a week travelling by train from London to Istanbul, my wife, friends Em and Phil, and I somehow arrived on schedule, glimpsing the sunrise as we pulled into the station. Everyone else crashed out at the hotel while I dashed off with my camera. Within minutes, I was holding my breakfast, from the street cart of one of the city's 1,400 registered simitçi. Simit are the definitive Turkish street food, traditionally eaten very fresh with a glass of black tea.

MAKES: 8–10

FROM MIXING TO OVEN: overnight plus 1½–2½ hours

BAKING TIME: 10–15 minutes

1. Mix the dough ingredients together thoroughly. Cover and leave to rest for 10 minutes.

2. Knead until smooth: as you are using a lower-protein flour, it won't be as stretchy as bread dough. Cover and leave to prove at room temperature for 30 minutes, then transfer to the refrigerator and leave overnight to continue proving.

3. Mix the pekmez and water together in a bowl and put the sesame seeds on a plate. Press the dough out on a lightly floured work surface, to de-gas the dough (that is, to get rid of the largest bubbles), so the finished product has an even texture.

4. Divide the dough into 8–10 equal-size pieces, rolling each one into a strand about 70–80cm/28–32in long. You might need to do this in two stages with a 5–10-minute rest in between. Hold the 2 ends of a strand together in one hand, and the middle in your other hand, and twist the dough a couple of times, to entwine the strands fully.

5. Pinch the ends of the twisted dough together to make a ring, then roll the join back and forth on a work surface a few times to seal fully. Repeat with the remaining strands of dough.

6. Dunk each simit into the diluted pekmez, then drain and dip into the sesame seeds to coat fully. Lay them out on two or three baking sheets, cover and leave to prove at room temperature for 30–45 minutes.

7. Heat the oven to 220°C/200°C fan/425°F/gas 7. Bake the simit for 10–15 minutes until reddish brown.

FOR THE DOUGH:
500g/1lb 2oz/3¾ cups plain/
　all-purpose flour
310g/11oz/1¼ cups plus 1 tbsp water
5g/1 tsp fresh yeast
5g/1 tsp fine/table salt

FOR THE COATING:
60g/2¼oz/scant ¼ cup pekmez
　(grape molasses)
50g/1¾oz/3½ tbsp water
200g/7oz/scant 1½ cups sesame seeds

Baker's Tip: Pekmez is a molasses-like syrup made by boiling down grape must. It can be bought from Turkish and Mediterranean shops and online.

Lahmacun DAVID JONES

Sometimes called Turkish or Armenian pizza, David says, "This works brilliantly in our wood-fired ovens, but will cook perfectly in a conventional one. It's different every time we make it, depending on what's available, so I like to think of this recipe as a wonderful inspiration, rather than something to be adhered to slavishly." Though he notes that using lemon and parsley "really brings it to life, so don't be tempted to skip that bit".

MAKES: 4 lahmacun
FROM MIXING TO OVEN: 5 hours
BAKING TIME: 5 minutes each

FOR THE DOUGH:
300g/10½oz/2 cups plus 2 tbsp white bread flour
100g/3½oz/¾ cup minus ½ tbsp wholemeal/wholewheat bread flour
8g/1½ tsp fresh yeast
5g/1 tsp fine/table salt
250g/9oz/1 cup plus 1 tbsp water

FOR THE TOPPING:
1 onion
1 carrot
1 large garlic clove
1 red pepper, deseeded
1 large tomato
1 handful of parsley leaves
½ tsp ground cumin
½ tsp ground coriander
1 tsp sumac
½ tsp dried chilli/red pepper flakes (optional)
250g/9oz/heaping 1 cup minced/ground lamb
salt and freshly ground black pepper

TO SERVE:
1 chilli, finely sliced (optional)
1 red onion, finely sliced
1 lemon
plain yogurt
1 handful of parsley leaves, chopped

1. Put both types of flour in a bowl, crumble in the yeast and then add the salt and water. Mix thoroughly, then knead for 10–15 minutes to create a strong and springy dough. Cover the bowl and leave at room temperature. After 2 hours, punch the dough once or twice, then firmly knead and fold it in on itself, to de-gas it. Leave for another 2 hours.

2. Meanwhile, blitz the onion, carrot, garlic, red pepper, tomato and parsley by pulsing in a food processor until chopped finely but not pulped.

3. Drain the excess liquid from the vegetables, either by pressing them in a sieve/strainer, or by wrapping in a clean cloth and squeezing the moisture out, then mix them with the rest of the topping ingredients in a large bowl, washing your hands well after handling the raw meat. This can be done ahead of time and refrigerated until needed.

4. Heat the oven to 220°C/200°C fan/425°F/gas 7, with baking stones or baking sheets in place. Divide the dough into 4 equal-size pieces, shape into balls, cover and leave to relax for 30 minutes.

5. Dust a rolling pin and the work surface with flour then roll the dough out into oval shapes about 2–3mm/up to ⅛in thick. Spoon the topping evenly over the 4 pieces of dough, spreading it out and pressing it in a little as you go, and folding the edges up and over slightly.

6. Using a floured peel, slide each lahmacun onto a baking stone and bake for about 5 minutes. You want them to cook thoroughly and the topping to take on a little colour, but without the bases crisping. Top each lahmacun with sliced chilli and onion, a good squeeze of lemon juice, a dollop of yogurt and a generous sprinkling of parsley. Serve immediately.

Bialys LIZ WEISBERG

These distant relatives of the bagel originated in Białystok, in an area of Russia that in 1918 became part of Poland. Historically, a high percentage of the city's population were Jewish, who as emigrants took their *bialys* wherever they went. Liz says, "A *bialy* is definitely *not* a bagel and is not made with bagel dough, although some bakeries make them that way. It is not boiled and, at its most original, it is dark and blistered, rather than pale and soft."

MAKES: 9 bialys
FROM MIXING TO OVEN: 5–6 hours
BAKING TIME: 20 minutes

FOR THE DOUGH:
500g/1lb 2oz/3½ cups white bread flour
325g/11½oz/1⅓ cups water
8g/1½ tsp fresh yeast
8g/1½ tsp fine/table salt

FOR THE TOPPING:
1 onion, finely minced
20g/¾oz/¼ cup dried breadcrumbs
poppy seeds, for sprinkling

semolina, for dusting

1. Mix the dough ingredients together thoroughly, then knead to form a smooth dough. This is a very "tight" (dry or stiff) dough, so you might find it easier to work in several short bursts, covering and leaving it to rest for about 10 minutes between each knead.

2. After kneading, cover the dough and leave to rise at room temperature for about 1½ hours, then give it a single fold, cover and leave for a further 2½ hours.

3. Divide the dough into 9 equal-size pieces, shape into balls and flatten to discs about 1cm/½in thick, resting the dough after shaping if it feels stiff. Cover and leave to rise at room temperature for 30 minutes.

4. Heat the oven to 220°C/200°C fan/425°F/gas 7, with a baking stone in place if you are not using a baking sheet. Meanwhile, mix the onion with the breadcrumbs.

5. Place the bialys on a baking sheet or a semolina-dusted peel, and make a very deep dimple 2.5cm/1in wide in the middle of each one by pressing down very firmly with your thumb. Smear a scant teaspoon of the topping into each dimple, spray or brush the bialys with water and sprinkle with poppy seeds. Slide the bialys into the oven and bake for 20 minutes, or until golden brown.

Liz Weisberg was born in Boston, USA, and life took her toward Battersea in London. There she and her partner Rachel Duffield set up The Lighthouse Bakery in 2000. After seven years, they upped sticks to the rolling hills of the High Weald in East Sussex, relaunching the business as a small wholesale bakery and baking school. Offering expertise and experience, their intention is to inspire a new generation of bakers.

Lihapiirakka CHRIS YOUNG

There are several recipes in this book for which there is really no excuse. They are unhealthy and just plain wrong. This is one of them. I first stumbled across these meat doughnuts (the literal translation is "meat pie") on a night out in Helsinki, Finland. By 3am, we were in need of refuelling, which came from a street-corner grilli van selling *lihis*, with added fried egg, frankfurter-style sausages, pickles, ketchup, mustard and (unusually) garlic sauce. Utter filth.

MAKES: 6 doughnuts
FROM MIXING TO COOKING: overnight plus 3½–4½ hours
COOKING TIME: 20–25 minutes

1. Beat the flour, water, egg, sugar and yeast together, ideally using a stand mixer with a dough hook, to make a smooth, stretchy dough. Add the salt and butter and knead until fully incorporated. Cover and leave in the refrigerator overnight.

2. Remove the dough from the refrigerator and leave to rise at room temperature for 2 hours. Meanwhile, fry the onion in a little oil until translucent, add the beef and salt and pepper to taste and remove from the heat.

3. Cook the rice, draining it if necessary, and cooling it quickly in a shallow layer on a large plate. When it is dry and fluffy, stir it into the onion and meat. Cool and refrigerate the filling until needed.

4. Divide the dough into 6 equal-size pieces, shape into balls, cover and leave to rest for 10 minutes. Dust the work surface and rolling pin with flour then roll out each dough ball into a circle about 15–18cm/ 6–7in in diameter and 1cm/½in thick.

5. Divide the filling evenly between the dough pieces, spreading it out but leaving a clean 1cm/½in border all the way round. Brush this clean edge with a little water or milk, fold the dough in half over the filling to make a semicircular shape and press down to seal. Cover and leave to rise for 1–2 hours.

6. In a deep, heavy pan, heat the vegetable oil to 180°C/350°F and fry 2 lihis at a time for 3–4 minutes on each side. Remove with a slotted metal spoon and leave to cool on a wire rack covered in paper towels while you fry the remaining "pies". Serve while still warm.

FOR THE DOUGH:
250g/9oz/1¾ cups plus 2 tbsp plain/ all-purpose flour
150g/5½oz/scant ⅔ cup water or milk
1 egg
10g/2 tbsp caster/superfine sugar
5g/1 tsp fresh yeast
4g/¾ tsp fine/table salt
30g/1oz/2 tbsp butter, softened

FOR THE FILLING:
½ onion, finely diced
vegetable oil for frying and deep frying
100g/3½oz/scant ½ cup minced/ ground beef
salt and freshly ground black pepper
50g/1¾oz/¼ cup long-grain white rice
a little water or milk

Baker's Tip: On second thoughts, leave this to the experts. Go to Helsinki and bag your *lihis* in their natural habitat of the bright orange Toripojat coffee tent in the city's harbourside market.

Pulla CHRIS YOUNG

According to some reports, the Finns drink more coffee per person than any other nationality. Whether or not that's true I've no idea, but my personal experience is that they guzzle *kahvia* as often as we Brits down tea. In someone's home, a cup will usually be accompanied by a cake or pastry, and more often than not that will be *pulla*.

MAKES: 12 pulla
FROM MIXING TO OVEN: overnight plus 1½ hours
BAKING TIME: 10–15 minutes

1. Crush the cardamom pods in a mortar and pestle, discard the husks and grind the seeds.

2. Rub the yeast and butter into the flour, then add the milk, egg, sugar, salt and cardamom seeds and mix thoroughly. Cover the dough and leave to rise slowly in the refrigerator overnight.

3. Grease a large baking sheet with butter. Divide the dough into 12 equal-size pieces, shape each piece into a ball and place on the baking sheet, 5cm/2in apart. Cover and leave to rise at room temperature for about 1 hour.

4. Heat the oven to 200°C/180°C fan/400°F/gas 6. Brush the top of each pulla with beaten egg and bake for 10–15 minutes until golden-brown.

15 green cardamom pods
5g/1 tsp fresh yeast
50g/1¾oz/3½ tbsp butter, softened, plus extra for greasing
500g/1lb 2oz/3¾ cups plain/all-purpose flour
300g/10½oz/1¼ cups milk
1 egg, beaten
80g/2¾oz/scant ½ cup caster/superfine sugar
5g/1 tsp fine/table salt
1 egg, beaten, for glazing

Sippet: At Lent, the *pulla* is pimped to become *laskiaispulla* by slicing off the top, spreading with jam/conserve and whipped cream and putting the top back on. In other Nordic countries, a sweetened almond paste is used instead of jam/conserve.

Cinnamon and Hazelnut Knots

CHRIS YOUNG

MAKES: 8 buns
FROM MIXING TO OVEN: 4½–6½ hours
BAKING TIME: 15–20 minutes

Back in early 2010, I spent two nights at Fifteen, the enterprise set up by Jamie Oliver to help train young people who have the passion to work in a high-end restaurant but who have struggled to hold down, or even find, a job. I was there to see what other bakeries could learn about taking on apprentices, and these buns are inspired by a loaf their baker Kenny Rankin showed me how to make, as well as by the spiced, enriched buns found across Scandinavia.

FOR THE DOUGH:
250g/9oz/1¾ cups white bread flour
100g/3½oz/¾ cup plain/all-purpose flour
140g/5oz/generous ½ cup buttermilk
40g/1½oz/¼ cup caster/superfine sugar
30g/1oz/2 tbsp butter
10g/2 tsp fresh yeast
1 egg
5g/1 tsp fine/table salt

FOR THE FILLING:
100g/3½oz/1¾ cups fresh white breadcrumbs, very fine
100g/3½oz/heaping ½ cup caster/superfine sugar
100g/3½oz/⅔ cup ground hazelnuts
4g/1½ tsp ground cinnamon
75g/2½oz/scant ½ cup water

icing/confectioners' sugar, for glazing

1. Mix all of the dough ingredients together thoroughly, then knead until you have a smooth, silky, stretchy dough. Cover and leave at room temperature for 3–5 hours until well risen.

2. Meanwhile, mix the filling ingredients together, adding the water a little at a time until you have a spreadable paste (you may not need it all). Cover and leave in the refrigerator until needed. Line a baking sheet with non-stick baking parchment.

3. Roll the dough out on a lightly floured work surface into a 40x20cm/16x8in rectangle, with the long edges to the sides and a short edge facing you. Spread the filling over the half of the dough nearest to you, then fold the remaining dough towards you to cover this.

4. Cut the dough lengthways into 8 strips, stretching them out to 25–30cm/10–12in long. Take a strip and, holding one end in each hand, twist it to create a rope effect (fig. 1). Holding one end firmly between thumb and forefinger, wrap the rest of the strip around twice (fig. 2), finishing by tucking the end of the strip into the middle of the spiral you have just created (fig. 3). Place on the lined baking sheet and repeat with the remaining strips of dough. Cover and leave to rise for 1 hour.

5. Heat the oven to 200°C/180°C fan/400°F/gas 6. Bake the knots for 10 minutes, then turn the oven down to 180°C/160°C fan/350°F/gas 4 and continue to bake for a further 5–10 minutes until golden brown. Leave to cool on a wire rack for 5–10 minutes, glazing the knots while still warm by brushing with water and dusting with icing/confectioners' sugar through a small sieve/strainer.

Rowies (Butteries) CHRIS YOUNG

Two names for basically the same thing: made with a laminated dough, these rolls could be considered the Scottish croissant. Using a technique akin to that for rough puff pastry leaves some fat in tiny pieces between the layers of dough, which bakes to a crisper finish, like the rowie of Aberdeen itself. Cutting the fat into the dough for an extra few minutes will give a softer result after baking: the butteries of the surrounding rural shires.

MAKES: 9–12 depending on size
FROM MIXING TO OVEN: overnight plus 3–4 hours
BAKING TIME: 15–20 minutes

350g/12oz/2½ cups white bread flour
250g/9oz/1 cup plus 1 tbsp water
5g/1 tsp fresh yeast
6g/1 tsp fine/table salt
60g/2¼oz/4 tbsp butter, at room temperature
100g/3½oz/½ cup minus 1 tbsp pork lard or beef dripping, at room temperature

1. Mix the flour, water, yeast and salt together thoroughly. Cover and leave to rest for 10 minutes then knead the dough until it is smooth and stretchy. Cover and leave at room temperature for 30 minutes, then leave in the refrigerator overnight.

2. The next day, beat the butter and lard together with a wooden spoon, balloon whisk or electric hand whisk until they are well whipped, pale and fluffy.

3. Dust the work surface and a rolling pin well with flour then roll the dough out into a rectangle about 1cm/½in thick. Spread it with about one-third of the whipped fat, then lift the dough by its left-hand edge, folding one-third of it over to cover the middle of the dough, then folding the right-hand side over this to leave a layered "parcel" one-third its previous width. Cover and leave in the refrigerator for 30 minutes.

4. Roll the dough out into a rectangle again, spread it with half the remaining fat and repeat the folding-in. Cover and return to the refrigerator for another 30 minutes, then roll the dough out for a third time, spreading it with the remaining fat and folding-in as before. Cover and return to the refrigerator for a final 30 minutes of chilling.

5. Dust the work surface and rolling pin well with flour, then roll the dough out to a rectangle about 1cm/½in thick. Cut or tear the dough into small rectangles or rounds, 65–85g/2¼–3oz in weight, or roughly 5cm/2in square. Place on baking sheets, leaving space for them to rise – they won't double in height, but will look noticeably larger. Cover and leave at room temperature for 1–2 hours.

6. Heat the oven to 220°C/200°C fan/425°F/gas 7. Bake the rowies for 15–20 minutes until risen and pale golden.

Staffordshire Oatcakes CHRIS YOUNG

The oatcakes of Staffordshire, Derbyshire and Cheshire are soft and almost like crêpes or pancakes. When I was young they rarely strayed to south Staffordshire where my family lived, but my dad's job used to take him to their native territory and he'd buy some. Now that I live in London, he still brings them to stock up my freezer when he visits. Here's my recipe, which uses yeast rather than the baking powder typically used by commercial producers.

MAKES: about 5 23cm/9in oatcakes

FROM MIXING TO COOKING: 4–5 hours, or overnight plus 1 hour

COOKING TIME: 3–4 minutes each

150g/5½oz/1½ cups rolled oats or oatmeal

50g/1¾oz/heaping ⅓ cup wholemeal/wholewheat flour

2g/½ tsp fresh yeast

300–350g/10½–12oz/1¼–1½ cups milk, water or mixture of the two

2g/½ tsp fine/table salt

a little butter or oil, for greasing

1. If using oats, put them into a food processor or upright blender and pulse them for 1–2 minutes until they take on a finer consistency. Mix all of the ingredients together in a bowl, cover and leave in the refrigerator overnight. Ideally, take the batter out again 1 hour before you need it: you can get away with using it very cold, but as the bubbles won't have got up to full force, the oatcake texture isn't quite as good.

2. If you want to do everything on the same day, leave the batter at room temperature for about 4–5 hours until bubbly. It should be about the consistency of house paint, but add a little more milk or water if it has thickened too much.

3. Assuming you don't have access to a baxton (a traditional oatcake griddle) lightly grease a flat, heavy frying pan, ideally about 25–30cm/10–12in in diameter, and place over a medium heat. Ladle in the batter and swirl around to form a pancake about 2–3mm/up to ⅛in thick.

4. Cook until the batter sets and bubbles burst through the surface like those in a crumpet or pikelet. Flip the oatcake over with a spatula or fish slice and cook for about another 2 minutes, checking to make sure it doesn't burn. Transfer to a plate and repeat until you have used up all the remaining batter.

Now, take a bite and tell me you're not a convert . . .

Baker's Tip: If you don't plan to eat all of the oatcakes within 24 hours (what's wrong with you?) put them on a wire cooling rack covered with a clean cloth until they are cool, layer between sheets of baking parchment to prevent them from sticking, seal in a plastic bag and freeze.

Sam Cutter is the head baker at Two Magpies Bakery, which opened in Southwold, Suffolk, in April 2013. The open-plan Scandinavian-style bakery and café makes a range of Real Bread using traditional methods. Bakery owner Rebecca Bishop says, "Demand for our long-fermented sourdough bread has grown massively and our customers love to watch us mixing, scaling and shaping each day's dough."

Brioche Doughnuts with Passionfruit Cream SAM CUTTER

MAKES: 10 doughnuts

FROM MIXING TO COOKING: overnight plus 3½–4 hours

COOKING TIME: 10–12 minutes, plus 10 minutes for filling

Deep-fried food isn't the usual territory of the Real Bread Campaign and this, like other enriched doughs in this book, should be viewed as an occasional indulgence. Sam originally created this dough to make burger buns for the local pub. He says he "tried it as a doughnut at a later date and discovered that it worked very well!"

FOR THE DOUGH:

6g/2 tsp osmotolerant dried yeast

70g/2½oz/¼ cup plus 2 tsp tepid water

280g/10oz/2 cups white bread flour

70g/2½oz beaten egg (about 1½ eggs)

45g/1½oz/3 tbsp butter, cut into cubes

5g/1 tsp fine/table salt

25g/1oz/scant 2 tbsp caster/superfine sugar

FOR THE FILLING:

125g/4½oz/½ cup passionfruit juice, fresh or frozen

125g/4½oz/scant ¾ cup caster/superfine sugar

2 large eggs plus 40g/1¼oz beaten egg yolk (about 2 yolks)

pinch of salt

125g/4½oz/9 tbsp unsalted butter, softened

140g/5oz/⅔ cup double/heavy cream

vegetable oil, for deep-frying

granulated sugar, for dusting

Baker's Tip: Osmotolerant yeast is designed especially for sugary doughs. If you can't find it, then use double the weight of fresh yeast.

1. Dissolve the yeast in the water. Add the flour and egg and mix well, then knead the dough until smooth and stretchy. Work the butter and salt in until thoroughly combined and the dough is silky again, then add the sugar and knead for a few more minutes until the dough no longer feels sticky or gritty. Cover the dough and leave to rise slowly in the refrigerator for 12–14 hours (typically overnight).

2. Grease a piece of baking parchment. Divide the dough into 10 equal-size pieces, shape them into small balls and place them seam-side down on the baking parchment, 5cm/2in apart. Cover and leave to rise at room temperature for 3–3½ hours until doubled in size.

3. Place a heat-resistant bowl over a saucepan half-filled with boiling water, so the water is not touching the bowl and adjust the heat so that the water continues to barely simmer. Put all the filling ingredients except the butter and cream into the bowl and stir constantly until the mixture is thick enough to coat the back of a spoon. Remove the bowl from the pan and stir in the butter until melted. Place this mixture in a clean container, cover the surface with clingfilm/plastic wrap to prevent a skin forming and leave to cool and set at room temperature, then whip it with the cream until thickened.

4. In a deep, heavy pan, heat the vegetable oil to 180–190°C/350–375°F. Lower several dough balls into the oil and fry for about 2 minutes on each side. Remove with a slotted metal spoon, drain off the excess oil, then roll them in the granulated sugar and leave to cool on a wire cooling rack while you fry the remaining balls of dough.

5. Push a small, serrated knife into the side of a doughnut and cut an upside-down "V" shape. Place the filling in a piping/pastry bag with a plain nozzle/tip, push it well into the cut and fill the doughnut until it starts to expand slightly. Repeat to fill the remaining doughnuts.

Croissants MICKAEL JAHAN

MAKES: 12 croissants

FROM MIXING TO OVEN: overnight
plus 4½–5 hours

BAKING TIME: 15–20 minutes .

A genuine, buttery, hand-laminated croissant is an increasingly rare pleasure, but not one beyond the enthusiastic home baker. August Zang's Viennese bakery brought the crescent-shaped Austrian *kipferl* to Paris in the late 1830s, and while this is generally accepted as the ancestor of the croissant, the first written recipe to create this butter-laminated dough apparently dates to just the early 20th century. Make sure you use high fat content butter, ideally 84%.

FOR THE DOUGH:

500g/1lb 2oz/3½ cups white bread
flour

240g/8½oz/1 cup water, as cold
as possible

9g/1½ tsp fine/table salt

15g/½oz/3 tbsp milk powder

20g/¾oz/4 tsp fresh yeast

60g/2oz/¼ cup caster/superfine sugar

FOR ROLLING OUT:

225g/8oz/1 cup butter, chilled

1 or 2 eggs, beaten, for glazing

1. Mix all the dough ingredients together very thoroughly (if you have a powerful stand mixer with a dough hook, start on slow, then speed up a little), until the dough is utterly smooth.

2. Shape the dough into a 25x12.5cm/10x5in rectangle on a floured work surface, then wrap it in clingfilm/plastic wrap. Roll the butter into a 12.5x12.5cm/5x5in square between two sheets of clingfilm/plastic wrap and refrigerate both the dough and the butter overnight.

3. Take the butter out of the refrigerator 1 hour before the dough, so it becomes pliable. Place the dough on a lightly-floured surface, then put the butter in the centre, sides lined up. Fold the uncovered dough at each end over the butter, so the edges meet but do not overlap.

4. Give the dough a quarter turn, then roll it out from the middle away and towards you, to seal the dough and butter together. When you have an elongated rectangle 5–7mm/¼in thick, fold the third furthest from you in to cover the middle portion, then the third nearest to you over that, to form an even, layered parcel. Cover the dough and chill it in the refrigerator for 15 minutes. Repeat the quarter turn, roll, fold and chill twice more, ending with 1 hour in the refrigerator.

5. Roll the dough out to a rectangle measuring 45x20cm/18x8in and about 3mm/⅛in thick. Slicing across the width of the rectangle, cut the dough into 12 elongated triangles, 7.5cm/3in at the base and 20cm/8in long. Cut a small nick in the middle of each base, then roll each croissant up from the base of the triangle towards the tip.

6. Place the croissants on baking sheets lined with non-stick baking parchment and brush with beaten egg. Prove for about 1¼ hours, ideally at around 28°C/82–83°F, or until well risen.

7. Heat the oven to 190°C/170°C fan/375°F/gas 5. Brush the croissants with egg again and bake for 15–20 minutes, or until golden brown. Transfer to a wire cooling rack to cool.

Mickael Jahan has been baking for over 25 years, starting in his home village of Vendee, France, when he was under 14 years old. In 1998 he landed in London and within three days found work at Sally Clarke's Bakery, one of the UK pioneers of the current Real Bread movement. Since graduating from the Institute National De La Boulangerie Pâtisserie, he has worked in every type of bakery of every size in both the UK and France.

Katie Venner and Gordon Woodcock built a brick oven and a bakery shed behind their home in rural Somerset in 2009 and started baking sourdough and other long-ferment Real Bread for friends and neighbours. This became the Tracebridge Sourdough microbakery, selling at local farmers' markets. They also run classes, pizza nights and welcome WOOF (World Wide Opportunities on Organic Farms) voluntary apprentices.

Appley Village Buns KATIE VENNER

These buns get their name not because they're made with apples (they're not: the filling is apricots) but because Katie first made them for the reopening of the local shop in her neighbouring Somerset village of Appley. They later inspired the Appley Bun Fun Run. If you wanted to make the buns more closely match their name, using chunks of peeled Bramley (cooking) apple instead of apricots might work rather well . . .

MAKES: 9 buns

FROM MIXING TO OVEN: 6–8 hours, or overnight plus 2–3 hours

BAKING TIME: 20 minutes

1. Mix the milk and yeast together, then add the flour, sugar, butter, salt and about half the beaten egg and knead until you have a smooth and stretchy dough. Cover and leave to rise at room temperature for 4–5 hours, or in the refrigerator overnight.

2. Shape the dough into a ball, cover and leave to rest while you make the custard. Whisk the cornflour/cornstarch, egg yolks and sugar together in a large bowl. Heat the milk to boiling point, then slowly pour it into the egg mixture, whisking continuously. Return the mixture to the pan and continue to whisk gently over a moderate heat until it thickens, being careful not to make it scramble. Remove from the heat, stir in the butter and vanilla, then leave to cool.

3. Lightly flour the work surface and a rolling pin, then roll the dough out into a rectangle about 50x30cm/20x12in. Spread with the cooled custard, right up to the edges, and then dot evenly with the apricots, orange zest and nutmeg.

4. Line a square baking tin with non-stick baking parchment. Roll the dough up lengthways like a Swiss/jelly roll, and cut it into 9 equal-size pieces. Arrange them together, cut side up, in the baking tin in rows of three. Cover and leave to rise at room temperature for about 1 hour.

5. Heat the oven to 190°C/170°C fan/375°F/gas 5. Brush the tops of the buns lightly with the remaining beaten egg left over from the dough. Sprinkle the almonds on top. Bake for 20 minutes, or until golden, then leave to cool slightly on a wire cooling rack.

6. Mix some icing/confectioners' sugar with just enough of the orange juice to make a thick ribbon of icing, then pipe it in a lattice pattern over the buns while they are still just warm.

FOR THE DOUGH:

125g/4½oz/½ cup milk, warm

12g/scant 2½ tsp fresh yeast

325g/11½oz/scant 2½ cups plain/all-purpose flour

50g/1¾oz/¼ cup caster/superfine sugar

60g/2¼oz/4 tbsp butter, softened

2½g/½ tsp fine/table salt

1 egg, beaten

FOR THE CUSTARD:

50g/1¾oz/½ cup cornflour/cornstarch

4 egg yolks

100g/3½oz/½ cup caster/superfine sugar

500g/1lb 2oz/2 cups milk

12g/2½ tsp butter

2½g/½ tsp pure vanilla extract

FOR THE FILLING:

100g/3½oz/⅔ cup chopped dried apricots, soaked and drained

zest of ½ unwaxed organic orange

a pinch of grated nutmeg

50g/1¾oz/scant ⅔ cup flaked/slivered almonds

FOR THE ICING:

icing/confectioners' sugar

juice of ½ orange

Devon Tuffs EMMA PARKIN

As they are made with baking powder, scones fall outside the Real Bread Campaign's area of interest, but here's a delicious and equally traditional alternative from South West England, made with baker's yeast. They are best served split, and spread with jam/conserve and clotted cream. The debate continues about the right way to do this, but Emma tells me that "east of the River Tamar, cream goes on first and jam on top!"

MAKES: 10–12 tuffs

FROM MIXING TO OVEN: 4½–5 hours

BAKING TIME: 12–15 minutes

280g/10oz/1¼ cups minus 1 tbsp milk, plus extra for glazing
15g/1 tbsp caster/superfine sugar
5g/1 tsp fresh yeast
450g/1lb/3¼ cups white bread flour
5g/1 tsp fine/table salt
30g/1oz/2 tbsp lard (or butter), plus extra for greasing

1. Warm the milk but not so hot you can't dip your finger in it. Cream together the sugar and yeast and mix with the milk.

2. Sift the flour and salt together, gently rub in the lard with your fingers or a fork to make fine crumbs, then add the yeast mixture. Knead for a minute or two until you have a consistent dough, but work it lightly to keep the finished tuffs quite "short" (even so, they won't be quite as crumbly as modern scones made with baking powder, which have no proving time and so no time for the gluten to develop).

3. Cover and leave to rise at room temperature for 3 hours until about doubled in size. Give the dough a single fold, cover again and leave to relax for 10 minutes.

4. Divide the dough into 10–12 equal-size pieces and shape them into balls. Alternatively, roll the dough out to about 1.5cm/⅝in thick and cut into circles with a pastry/cookie cutter. Lightly grease two baking sheets with lard, place the dough pieces on them about 5cm/2in apart, cover and leave to prove for 1 hour.

5. Heat the oven to 220°C/200°C fan/425°F/gas 7. Brush the top of each tuff with milk, then bake for about 12–15 minutes until golden brown.

Emma Parkin was born and bred in Exeter, Devon. Before founding Emma's Bread in 2005, her jobs included graphic designer (in the days before computers) and Soil Association press officer. Her bakery is at the heart of the Real Food Store, Exeter city-centre's community-owned local food shop. The bakery is clearly visible to customers, helping them understand the process, involvement of people and value of this daily essential.

Hot Cross Buns DUNCAN GLENDINNING

Spiced, fruited, enriched buns have a long history: as Elizabeth David noted, in 1592 the London Clerk of Markets restricted their sale to funerals, Christmas and Good Friday. The first reference to "hot cross buns" may be from as recently as 1733; today, industrial manufacturers in Britain mass produce what they call hot cross buns all year round. Duncan suggests serving them "toasted and smothered with butter, or simply enjoyed with a cup of tea".

MAKES: 10 buns
FROM MIXING TO OVEN: 4–5 hours, or overnight plus 1–2 hours
BAKING TIME: 15–20 minutes

1. Mix the flour, sugar, salt and spice together in a bowl and rub the softened butter in with your fingertips.

2. Crumble the yeast into the water, mix until dissolved and pour this yeasty water along with the milk and egg into the flour. Mix together thoroughly, then knead to make a soft, supple dough. Don't panic if it feels a little wetter and stickier than you're used to, just stay with it and keep kneading until you get there.

3. Gently work the mincemeat or dried fruit into the dough until distributed evenly without breaking the fruit up too much, which would leave dirty-looking streaks in the buns. Cover and leave to rise at room temperature for 3 hours, or in the refrigerator overnight.

4. Grease a baking sheet with butter. Cut the dough into 10 equal-size pieces, shape into balls and place on the baking sheet, about 5cm/2in apart so they can rise and grow without touching. Cover and leave to rise for 1–1½ hours, or until doubled in size.

5. Heat the oven to 190°C/170°C fan/375°F/gas 5. Mix together the paste ingredients and put into a piping/pastry bag. Brush the top of each bun with beaten egg and pipe a cross onto it. Bake the buns for 15–20 minutes until rich gold in colour.

Duncan Glendinning founded The Thoughtful Bread Company in 2008 and set up the bakery in a converted farm outbuilding the following year. The bakery and baking school later moved to the heart of Bath, where using ingredients they've grown themselves, foraged or bartered for with customers is not unknown. Duncan is one of the Real Bread Campaign's official ambassadors.

FOR THE DOUGH:
500g/1lb 2oz/3½ cups white bread flour
50g/1¾oz/¼ cup caster/superfine sugar
5g/1 tsp fine/table salt
2–3g/½–¾ tsp ground mixed spice/ pumpkin pie spice
75g/2½oz/5 tbsp butter, softened, plus extra for greasing
10g/2 tsp fresh yeast
90g/3¼oz/6 tbsp water
150g/5½oz/scant ⅔ cup milk
1 egg
175g/6oz/¾ cup fruit mincemeat or a mixture of dried fruits

FOR THE PASTE:
100g/3½oz/¾cup plain/all-purpose flour
30g/1oz/2 tbsp caster/superfine sugar
80g/2¾oz/⅓ cup milk

1 egg, beaten, for glazing

Baker's Tip: To add a wonderful shine and finger-licking stickiness, add a second glaze of icing/confectioners' sugar mixed with a dribble of water while the buns are still warm.

Earl Grey Tea Loaf DAVID JONES

David says, "This loaf has always been a winner and gets great feedback. If I don't make it our Bread of the Month two or three times a year, I start to get complaints." He adds that "if the end of a loaf is around long enough to go stale, try it lightly fried in a little butter and served with fruit compote and yogurt for breakfast. Knockout!" Make sure that the Earl Grey you use to brew the tea for this recipe is a classic blend, with natural bergamot flavouring.

MAKES: 1 loaf

FROM MIXING TO OVEN: overnight plus 5 hours

BAKING TIME: 25–30 minutes

FOR THE SOAKER:

125g/4½oz/½ cup Earl Grey tea, freshly brewed, hot, black and strong

50g/1¾oz/⅓ cup raisins

50g/1¾oz/¼ cup sultanas/golden raisins

FOR THE DOUGH:

350g/12oz/2½ cups white bread flour

5g/1 tsp fresh yeast

6g/1 tsp fine/table salt

1 medium egg

zest of 1 unwaxed organic lemon

50g/1¾oz/3½ tbsp butter, softened, plus extra for greasing

100g/3½oz/½ cup minus 1 tbsp milk

75g/2½oz/5 tbsp water

2–3g/½–¾ tsp ground mixed spice/ pumpkin pie spice

1 egg, beaten, for glazing

juice of ½ a lemon

8g/1½ tsp caster/superfine sugar

1. Pour the freshly brewed Earl Grey tea over the dried fruit in a bowl, cover and leave to soak overnight.

2. Next day, mix the dough ingredients together thoroughly, then turn the dough out onto the work surface and knead for 10–15 minutes until smooth and stretchy. The dough will be very sticky at first but should be just about dry to the touch by the time you finish kneading. Resist the temptation to add any more flour.

3. Drain the fruit, discarding the excess liquid, and add to the dough. Continue to knead until the fruit is well distributed but avoid breaking it up too much. Cover the dough and leave to rise at room temperature for 3 hours.

4. Give the dough a single fold, cover and leave to rest for 10 minutes. Meanwhile, grease a 1kg/2lb loaf tin with butter, then shape the dough to fit and place in the tin. Cover and leave at room temperature for about 1 hour.

5. Heat the oven to 210°C/190°C fan/415°F/gas 6–7. Brush the top of the dough with beaten egg. Bake for 15 minutes, then turn the oven down to 190°C/170°C fan/375°F/gas 5 and continue to bake for a further 10–15 minutes. The bread is cooked when a skewer inserted into the middle of the loaf comes out clean and dry. Turn the loaf out of the tin and leave to cool on a wire cooling rack.

6. Warm the lemon juice and caster/superfine sugar in a saucepan until dissolved and brush this over the warm loaf.

Baker's Tip: As an alternative to Earl Grey tea, you could try redbush (rooibos) or orange pekoe, each of which brings its own character.

David Jones and his wife Holly set up Manna from Devon Cooking School in 2006, running classes including baking Real Bread in a wood-fired oven. He also bakes for various food festivals and a monthly local bread delivery around the village.

Sourdough

The oldest (and some people would say still the best) way of leavening a loaf is by using a sourdough starter.

Yeasts and bacteria are found in the air, soil, water . . . basically everywhere. It might or might not be a coincidence that the surfaces of cereal grains tend to teem with types that are suited to bread making. After grinding the grains, some of these critters remain in the flour and by creating the right conditions you can nurture them into a thriving culture.

Eventually there will be enough yeast cells in the culture giving off carbon dioxide to make dough rise. At the same time, lactic acid bacteria will be producing lactic and acetic acids.

This all happens relatively slowly and over this longer fermentation time, acids, enzymes and by-products the microbes generate have beneficial effects on the flavour, texture and aroma of the finished bread. The processes can also have a natural preservative effect and might have health benefits, too.

Spelt Sourdough ANDREW AULD

Whatever anyone tells you, spelt is a type of wheat, though some people who struggle with eating bread wheat find that they are fine with spelt. Whether this is because of differences in the grains or the processes by which each is typically made into loaves is not yet determined. For the purposes of this book, all you really need to know is that spelt makes a relatively high-protein flour with plenty of nutty flavour, especially if you choose wholemeal/wholegrain.

MAKES: 2 small loaves

FROM MIXING TO OVEN: 16–18 hours, or overnight plus 4 hours

BAKING TIME: 40 minutes

FOR THE PRE-FERMENT:

60g/2¼oz/½ cup light spelt flour

60g/2¼oz/½ cup wholemeal/ wholegrain spelt flour

50g/1¾oz/3½ tbsp water

15g/½oz/1 tbsp rye sourdough starter

FOR THE DOUGH:

250g/9oz/2 cups light spelt flour

250g/9oz/2 cups wholemeal/ wholegrain spelt flour

300g/10½oz/1¼ cups water

50g/1¾oz/3½ tbsp orange juice

10g/2 tsp honey

7g/1½ tsp fine/table salt

1. Mix the pre-ferment ingredients together thoroughly, cover and leave at room temperature for 12–14 hours (typically overnight).

2. Mix the pre-ferment with the dough ingredients, then knead everything together until you have a smooth and stretchy dough. Cover and leave for 3 hours, giving the dough a single fold after 1 and 2 hours.

3. Divide the dough into 2 equal-size pieces and shape as desired. If using proving baskets, dust them well with flour and place the dough in them, seam-side up, though for flatter loaves you can simply leave the shaped dough on a floured work surface, seam-side down. Cover the dough and leave to prove for 1 hour.

4. Heat the oven to 240°C/220°C fan/475°F/gas 8–9, with a large baking stone or baking sheet in place.

5. Either turn the loaves out of their baskets, or carefully transfer them from the work surface, so they are seam-side down on a floured peel. Slide the loaves onto the baking stone and bake for 10 minutes, then turn the oven down to 200°C/180°C fan/400°F/gas 6 and continue to bake for a further 30 minutes. Remove from the oven and leave on a wire rack to cool.

Andrew Auld opened "the loaf" in 2008, reinvigorating a bakery that had been in the Derbyshire village of Crich since 1919. As well as offering Real Bread and other baked goodies, it acts as a community hub. The bakehouse is a place to meet, eat and socialize, while the bakers work with groups including the village primary school.

Michael Fahy and his wife Helen started The Island Bakers on the Isle of Wight in 2010 after Michael fell in love with making sourdough bread. Originally chefs, Michael and Helen found that they were not alone in wanting a supplier of Real Bread to complement the food they were serving. He says that this pumpkin bread is their most popular loaf throughout the autumn.

Roasted Pumpkin Sourdough

MICHAEL FAHY

The pumpkin or squash needs to be a firm-fleshed variety, rather than one of the big, woolly types best suited to Hallowe'en lanterns. Michael suggests Crown Prince winter squash, "because of the nutty flavour and robust flesh". Adding some pumpkin seeds gives extra texture, for the perfect loaf.

MAKES: 2 large loaves

FROM MIXING TO OVEN: 2 days plus 2 hours

BAKING TIME: 45–50 minutes

1. Mix the starter, both flours and the water for the pre-ferment together thoroughly, cover and leave at room temperature for 16–18 hours (typically overnight).

2. Heat the oven to 180°C/160°C fan/350°F/gas 4. Cut the pumpkin in half, scoop out the seeds and rub the flesh with oil and salt. Place the thyme stalks into the cavities of the pumpkin, put them cut-side down onto a greased baking sheet and roast for 1–2 hours, or until the pumpkin flesh is soft and has some caramelization. Leave to cool completely, then scoop the pumpkin flesh out in large chunks, reserving 200g/7oz of it for this recipe and discarding the skin (any spare pumpkin can be frozen for another time, or used in another recipe).

3. Next day, thoroughly mix the pre-ferment with the water and both flours for the dough. Cover and leave to rest for 30–60 minutes. Add the salt and knead for 2–4 minutes, then add the pumpkin flesh and seeds, scrunching them into the dough with wetted hands. Cover and leave to prove for 1 hour.

4. Turn the dough out onto the work surface and give it a single fold, return it to the bowl, cover and prove for a further 1 hour, or until the dough is light, bubbling and doubled in size.

5. Turn the dough onto the work surface, divide it into 2 equal-size pieces and shape into balls. Flour 2 proving baskets and place the dough in them, seam-side up. Cover and leave to prove in the refrigerator overnight, taking them out 1–2 hours before baking.

6. Heat the oven to 250°C/230°C fan/480°F/gas 9+, or as high as it will go, with a baking stone or baking sheet in place. Turn the loaves out onto a floured peel one at a time, then slide them onto the baking stone. Bake for 15 minutes, then turn the oven down to 200°C/180°C fan/400°F/gas 6, and continue to bake for another 30–35 minutes.

FOR THE PRE-FERMENT AND PUMPKIN:

5g/1 tsp white sourdough starter

100g/3½oz/¾ cup minus ½ tbsp white bread flour

15g/1¾ tbsp wholemeal/wholewheat bread flour

115g/4oz/½ cup water, at room temperature

1 small pumpkin or squash

vegetable oil, for brushing and greasing

salt flakes

thyme sprigs

FOR THE DOUGH:

310g/11oz/1¼ cups plus 1 tbsp water, at room temperature

450g/1lb/about 3¼ cups white bread flour

30g/1oz/scant 3½ tbsp wholemeal/ wholewheat bread flour

12g/2 tsp fine/table salt

100g/3½oz/¾ cup shelled pumpkin seeds, lightly toasted

Fig and Fennel Sourdough ROGER BIRT

MAKES: 1 large loaf

FROM MIXING TO OVEN: overnight plus 5 hours

BAKING TIME: 30 minutes

Roger chose to share this recipe as he feels "it epitomizes our ethos of producing great-tasting breads that encourage customers to try something different".

FOR THE PRE-FERMENT:

100g/3½oz/scant ½ cup white sourdough starter

75g/2½oz/½ cup plus ½ tbsp white bread flour

75g/2½oz/scant ⅓ cup water

FOR THE DOUGH:

350g/12oz/2½ cups white bread flour

150g/5½oz/1 cup wholemeal/wholewheat bread flour

300g/10½oz/1¼ cups water

10g/1 heaping tbsp green fennel seeds

10g/2 tsp fine/table salt

175g/6¼oz/scant 1¼ cups quartered dried figs

1. Mix the pre-ferment ingredients together thoroughly, cover and leave at room temperature for 12–14 hours (typically overnight).

2. To make the dough, add both flours with the water and fennel seeds to the pre-ferment, and mix thoroughly. Cover and leave to rest at room temperature for 20–30 minutes.

3. Mix in the salt and knead for a few minutes. Cover and leave to rest at room temperature for another 30 minutes.

4. Turn the dough out onto a lightly floured work surface, using a rolling pin to roll it out into a rectangle. Distribute the figs evenly over half the dough, then fold the other half over them, pressing the edges together to seal. Roll the dough out again, fold in half and roll out once more. If the figs are not evenly distributed, repeat the process but be careful not to mush them up completely.

5. Shape the dough into a ball, cover and leave to prove at room temperature for 1 hour.

6. Give the dough a single fold, cover and leave to prove for another 2 hours, or until almost doubled in size.

7. Dust a proving basket well with flour. Turn the dough out onto a lightly floured work surface and shape to fit the basket. Place the dough seam-side up in the basket, cover and leave to prove at room temperature for 1 hour.

8. Heat the oven to 230°C/210°C fan/450°F/gas 8, with a baking stone or baking sheet in place. Turn the dough out onto a peel and slide it onto the baking stone. Bake for 10 minutes, then turn the oven down to 200°C/180°C fan/400°F/gas 6 and bake for a further 20 minutes, checking halfway through that it is not browning too quickly.

Roger Birt and his wife Sally set up Red Dog Bakery in North Devon after successful non-food careers. They began to head down this path when the stomach cramps Roger experienced eating industrial loaves were non-existent when enjoying Real Bread. Roger began baking at home, went on courses and, inspired by David and Holly Jones at Manna from Devon, turned it into a business.

Seeded Wholemeal Sourdough

CRAIG SAMS

This loaf's roots reach back to Ceres, the organic bakery that Craig and his brother Greg Sams owned on Portobello Road in London's Notting Hill. In turn, Ceres was inspired by the *desem* baking of Omer Gevaert at the Lima bakery he founded in Ghent, Belgium, in 1963. The loaf continued to evolve when Craig and his wife Jo took over Judges Bakery in Hastings on England's south coast, with the addition of kelp granules and hemp, sesame and linseeds/flaxseeds.

MAKES: 1 large loaf
FROM MIXING TO OVEN: 4–7 hours
BAKING TIME: 30–40 minutes

400g/14oz/scant 3 cups wholemeal/ wholewheat bread flour

100g/3½oz/scant ½ cup wholemeal/ wholewheat sourdough starter

25g/1oz/heaping 2¾ tbsp sesame seeds

7g/1 tbsp hemp seeds, hulled

35g/1¼oz/¼ cup linseeds/flaxseeds

2g/½ tsp kelp granules or powder

8g/1½ tsp fine/table salt

300–330g/10½–11¾oz/1¼–1⅓ cups water

rolled oats, for topping

1. Mix all of the ingredients except the oats together thoroughly. Cover the dough and leave to rest for 10 minutes.

2. Knead the dough until smooth and stretchy, cover and leave to prove at room temperature for 1 hour.

3. Shape the dough to fit a large proving basket, lightly dampen the top of the dough with a little water, and roll it in the oats.

4. Dust the large proving basket well with flour and place the dough in it, seam-side up. Cover and leave to prove at room temperature for 3–6 hours or until doubled in size.

5. Heat the oven to 200°C/180°C fan/400°F/gas 6, with a baking stone or baking sheet in place. Turn the dough out onto a floured peel, seam-side down, slash the top, then slide it onto the baking stone and bake for 30–40 minutes.

Craig Sams has been a food pioneer in Britain since arriving from the USA in 1966. In 1968, he and brother Greg established macrobiotic restaurant Seed. This was followed by Ceres Grain Shop, Harmony Foods (later to become Whole Earth Foods), and in 1972, Ceres Bakery. With his wife Jo Fairley, Craig founded Green & Black's chocolate, producer of the UK's first Fairtrade certified product, and later moved to Judges Bakery in Hastings. He is chairman of Carbon Gold, a leading biochar company and Gusto Organic, producers of organic Fairtrade low-calorie cola.

Rye Sourdough ALEX GOOCH

By adding a slight bitter-sweetness with black treacle/molasses, Alex's variation on a basic rye sourdough gives your tastebuds a very pleasurable workout. This loaf goes very well with hard and blue artisan cheeses.

MAKES: 2 small loaves
FROM MIXING TO OVEN: 4½–5 hours
BAKING TIME: 45 minutes

1. Mix all of the dough ingredients together in a bowl to form a thick batter, cover and leave to rest for 30 minutes. Meanwhile, grease two 500g/1lb loaf tins.

2. Divide the batter evenly between the two loaf tins and lightly dust the top of each with rye flour. Cover and leave at room temperature for about 4 hours until risen to the top of the tins.

3. Heat the oven to 200°C/180°C fan/400°F/gas 6. Uncover the tins, dust the loaves with rye flour again and bake for 45 minutes.

4. Remove the loaves from the oven and turn out onto a wire cooling rack to cool. As rye loaves of this type are very sticky inside when just baked, the fully cooled loaves then need to be left in a bread bin or other suitable container for at least 4 hours and preferably a day or two before eating (if you can wait that long).

400g/14oz/scant 3⅔ cups light
    rye flour, plus extra for dusting
300g/10½oz/3¼ cups rye sourdough
    starter
330g/11¾oz/1⅓ cups water
50g/1¾oz/⅓ cup chopped rye grains
15g/1 tbsp black treacle/molasses
10g/2 tsp fine/table salt
butter, for greasing

Alex Gooch started his organic Real Bread bakery in 2007 with loans from family and friends. At first he worked hundred-hour weeks to establish the business, selling at festivals and food markets. In 2010 he was named Best Food Producer at the BBC Food & Farming Awards. Alex says "I've always been fascinated by bread. My absolute love and passion for it drove me on. Top-quality organic ingredients are essential. I work with many grains, including stoneground British heritage varieties."

Baker's Tip: For variety, you can add a small handful of seeds, chopped nuts or raisins or other dried fruit into the mixture.

Fergus Jackson and his wife Sharmin set up Brick House bakery in southeast London in April 2012 having grown tired of corporate life. His loaf learning includes stints at San Francisco Baking Institute, Tartine in the same city and E5 Bakehouse in London. Specializing in San Fran-style sourdoughs, his accolades include being noted as one of London's top 5 bakeries by *The Financial Times Weekend Magazine*.

The Shackleton FERGUS JACKSON

The polar explorer Sir Ernest Shackleton went to school in Dulwich, in the same part of London where Fergus now bakes. This recipe includes black treacle/molasses as a nod to the tins of golden syrup taken by the explorer on his expeditions, and Fergus says, "I like to think of this as the loaf he slipped into his backpack before heading off to the South Pole." It goes well with smoked fish, Marmite, goats' (chevre) or blue cheese, radishes and salt, or just butter.

MAKES: 1 large loaf

FROM MIXING TO OVEN: 6–7 hours

BAKING TIME: 50–60 minutes

1. Mix the soaker ingredients together and leave for at least 2 hours.

2. Mix all of the ingredients including the soaker together until thoroughly combined, to make a sticky, shaggy dough. Transfer this to a lightly oiled bowl, cover and leave to prove at room temperature for 45 minutes.

3. Give the dough a single fold, cover and leave to prove for a further 45 minutes.

4. Turn the dough out onto a lightly floured work surface, flatten it out and then shape it into a ball. Cover and allow to rest for 20 minutes.

5. Grease a 1kg/2lb loaf tin, shape the dough to fit and place it in the tin, seam-side down. Using a wet hand, press the dough down gently to fill out the tin into the corners and flatten the loaf's shape. Cover and leave to prove at room temperature for 2–3 hours. This is a fairly dense loaf so the dough will not rise dramatically during the final proving but you should see an increase in size and a gentle doming of the surface.

6. Heat the oven to 230°C/210°C fan/450°F/gas 8. Slash a line down the middle of the dough, place in the oven and bake for 50–60 minutes. Remove from the tin as soon as possible and leave to cool completely, ideally for 12 hours or more, before cutting.

FOR THE SOAKER:

75g/2½oz/heaping ¾ cup jumbo rolled oats

75g/2½oz/½ cup linseeds/flaxseeds

150g/5½oz/scant ⅔ cup water

FOR THE DOUGH:

170g/6oz/scant 1¼ cups wholemeal/ wholewheat bread flour

170g/6oz/1½ cups wholemeal/ wholegrain (dark) rye flour

85g/3oz/½ cup plus 1 tbsp white bread flour

205g/7¼oz/¾ cup plus 2 tbsp water

100g/3½oz/scant ½ cup wholemeal/ wholewheat or rye sourdough starter

45g/1½oz/generous 2 tbsp black treacle/molasses

10g/2 tsp fine/table salt

oil, for greasing

Beetroot Sourdough LAURA BULLOCK

Laura says that this loaf has "earthy flavours that are perfect with goats' cheese and mackerel". The beetroot/beet lends the white crumb an unusual burgundy colour; a simple variation would be to replace the beetroot/beet with grated carrot or parsnip, which will give an orange or creamy fleck to the crumb, depending on the vegetable used.

MAKES: 2 small loaves

FROM MIXING TO OVEN: 2½–3 hours
then overnight

BAKING TIME: 20–25 minutes each loaf

430g/15¼oz/3 cups white bread flour

100g/3½oz/scant ½ cup white
sourdough starter

8g/1½ tsp fine/table salt

250g/9oz/1 cup plus 1 tbsp water

330g/11½oz/scant 2¼ cups peeled
raw grated beetroot/beets

1. Mix the flour, sourdough starter, salt and most of the water together thoroughly. If the dough is too stiff, add more of the water. Knead the dough until smooth and stretchy, then cover and leave to rest for 10 minutes.

2. Flatten the dough out to form a rectangle. Scatter the beetroot/ beets over it and knead in until distributed evenly. The dough will be very soft and sticky. Shape into a ball, cover and leave to rest for 30 minutes.

3. Give the dough a single fold and rest for a further 30 minutes, then fold and rest for 30 minutes twice more.

4. Dust two 500g/1lb proving baskets with flour. Divide the dough into 2 equal-size pieces and shape to fit the baskets. Place the dough in the baskets seam-side up, cover and leave to prove in the refrigerator for 12 hours overnight.

5. Heat the oven to 250°C/230°C fan/480°F/gas 9+, or as high as your oven will go, with a baking stone or baking sheet in place. Turn one piece of dough out of its basket onto a floured peel and slash the top, then slide it onto the stone. Bake for 20 minutes, or 25 if you prefer a slightly darker crust. Repeat with the remaining piece of dough.

Laura Bullock and Matina Mitchell met at the School of Artisan Food, where they decided to set up their own bakery. Experience at a market in Sheffield during their course convinced them that there was the demand for a Real Bread bakery in the city. They launched Seven Hills Bakery in November 2011, and the team quickly grew from three to ten people in its first 18 months.

Victoria Osborne has been baking for about 20 years. She told me that she thinks her microbakery, Wraxall Real Bread, might be the smallest in Wiltshire. She bakes sourdoughs and other slowly proved breads, which include combinations like nettle and wild garlic, once a week to sell at a local country market.

Red Grape and Fennel Seed Schiacciata VICTORIA OSBORNE

This is Victoria's sourdough version of *schiacciata con l'uva*, a Tuscan member of the hearth-bread family that also includes *focaccia* and *fougasse*. Recipes often include rosemary, rather than fennel seeds, and may be topped with sugar instead of salt.

MAKES: 2 small loaves
FROM MIXING TO OVEN: overnight plus 3½–4 hours
BAKING TIME: 15–20 minutes

1. Mix the flour, semolina, starter, salt and water together thoroughly, until all of the ingredients have come together in a sticky mass with no dry bits remaining. Add the olive oil and work it gently into the dough. Place in a lightly oiled bowl, cover and leave to rest for 30 minutes.

2. Give the dough a single fold, cover and leave to rest for another 30 minutes.

3. Repeat this fold and rest process three more times, after which the dough should be very smooth and stretchy. Cover the dough again and leave in the refrigerator overnight.

4. Take the dough out of the refrigerator and leave for at least 1 hour to come up to room temperature. Turn the dough onto a lightly oiled work surface and divide it into 2 equal-size pieces. Gently shape each piece into a ball, cover and leave it to relax for 30 minutes.

5. Lightly flatten each piece of dough with the heel of your hand to form a circle, then place onto baking sheets lined with non-stick baking parchment. Cover and leave to prove for 2 hours.

6. Drizzle 1 tablespoon of oil over each piece of dough and lightly spread it across the surface. Squeeze the grapes gently until they break (*schiacciata* means "crushed") and press them deep into the dough. Sprinkle the tops with fennel seeds and salt to taste, then cover and leave to prove again while the oven heats up.

7. Heat the oven to 240°C/220°C fan/475°F/gas 8–9. Bake the loaves for 15–20 minutes, or until risen and pale golden.

500g/1lb 2oz/3½ cups white bread flour
20g/2 tbsp semolina
100g/3½oz/scant ½ cup rye sourdough starter
5g/1 tsp fine/table salt
300g/10½oz/1¼ cups tepid water
60g/2¼oz/generous ⅓ cup olive oil, plus 2 tbsp for drizzling
250g/9oz/2–2½ cups seedless red grapes

fennel seeds, for sprinkling
coarse sea salt flakes, for sprinkling

Pane di Patate PAOLO MAGAZZINI

Paolo is a professional baker in Garfagnana, in the province of Lucca, Italy. Made there, using particular flour, potatoes, methods and a wood-fired oven, this loaf is allowed to bear the name *Pane di Patate della Garfagnana* and is supported by a Slow Food Presidium. The tipo 1 flour used in this recipe is a creamy-to-beige-coloured *farina di grano tenero*, milled from "common" wheat rather than the *grano duro* (durum wheat) used more often for pasta.

MAKES: 1 large loaf
FROM MIXING TO OVEN: 4–8 hours
BAKING TIME: 1 hour

100g/3½oz/scant ½ cup mashed potato, a floury/starchy variety

310g/11oz/3 cups tipo 1 flour

310g/11oz/2½ cups wholemeal/ wholegrain emmer flour (Italian farro, *Triticum dicoccum*)

10g/2 tsp fine/table salt

100g/3½oz/scant ½ cup white sourdough starter

370g/13oz/1½ cups plus 1 tbsp cooking water, reserved from boiling the potatoes (at 38–40°C/ 100–105°F)

fine polenta flour/cornmeal, for dusting

1. Peel, boil, drain and mash the potato, reserving the cooking water. Measure out the amount of mashed potato required for the recipe, setting any leftovers aside for another purpose. Mix the potato and all of the other dough ingredients together thoroughly, then knead the dough until it is smooth and stretchy. Cover and leave to rest for 10 minutes.

2. Dust a large proving basket with fine polenta flour/cornmeal. Shape the dough into a ball, roll the seam-side in fine polenta flour/cornmeal and place seam-side up in the basket. Cover and leave to prove at room temperature for 4–8 hours.

3. Heat the oven to 250°C/230°C fan/480°F/gas 9+, or as high as it will go, with a baking stone or baking sheet in place. Turn the dough out, seam-side down, onto a polenta/cornmeal-dusted peel and slide onto the baking stone. Bake for 15 minutes, then turn the heat down to 200°C/180°C fan/400°F/gas 6 and continue to bake for another 45 minutes.

Baker's Tip: Despite what the literal translations of the Italian names might suggest, the flour you are using here is bread making flour, not a "soft" plain/all purpose flour.

Paolo Magazzini is a farro and beef farmer and the baker in Petrognola, Tuscany. His mother was the village baker until she died in 2000. Seeing his mother's sadness that her bread wouldn't live on, Paolo promised he would continue to bake it. As well as her recipes, he still uses her *madre* (sourdough starter) that has been kept alive for more than 50 years.

Elderflower Sourdough JOE FITZMAURICE

Elder (*Sambucus nigra*) grows across Europe like a weed. When foraging for elderflowers, avoid any near roads or that may have been sprayed with herbicides or pesticides. To prepare them, brush and shake off any dirt and insects, and discard all but the smallest part of the stalk. Don't wash the flowers as they will lose much of their scent and flavour. Make sure that you are gathering *Sambucus nigra*, as other members of the genus are considered to be toxic.

MAKES: 2 large loaves

FROM MIXING TO OVEN: 5 hours

BAKING TIME: 30–35 minutes

1. Mix the flour, the starter and all but 20g/4 tsp of the water together thoroughly, then knead the dough for a few minutes. Cover and leave to rest for about 20 minutes.

2. Stretch the dough out on the work surface, sprinkle with the salt and remaining water and knead until you have a smooth and stretchy dough.

3. Gently knead the elderflowers into the dough until they are evenly distributed, then divide the dough into 2 equal-size pieces, shape into balls, cover and leave to rest at room temperature for about 10 minutes.

4. Dust two large proving baskets generously with flour. Shape the dough balls to fit the baskets and place them in, seam-side up. Cover and leave to prove at room temperature for about 4 hours. To get large, uneven holes in the crumb and good oven spring, Joe suggests that the dough should be placed in the oven slightly under-proved.

5. Heat the oven to 220°C/200°C fan/425°F/gas 7, with a baking stone or baking sheet in place. Turn 1 loaf out onto a floured peel, slash the top and slide it onto the baking stone, then repeat with the second loaf. Bake for 20 minutes, check on how the loaves are progressing, then continue to bake for another 10–15 minutes until done.

710g/1lb 9oz/5 cups white bread flour
210g/7½oz/scant 1 cup white sourdough starter
490g/1lb 1¼oz/2 cups water
15g/3 tsp fine/table salt
35g/1¼oz elderflowers, cleaned

Joe Fitzmaurice began baking professionally at his sisters' Dublin deli in 2000, before they opened a bakery together in 2004. In 2008, he and his wife moved to County Tipperary, where he built a wood-fired oven and set up the certified organic Cloughjordan Bakery, which evolved into his current bakery Riot Rye. In 2015, Joe became a founder member of Real Bread Ireland on a mission to share the delights of sourdough in the land of soda loaves or farls.

Baker's Tip: For a very different loaf, replace the elderflowers with 30g/1oz/scant ¼ cup chopped toasted hazelnuts, 40g/1½oz/2 tbsp honey and some fresh lavender flowers stripped off their stalks, and reduce the water by 40g/1½oz/scant 3 tbsp.

Hairst Breid JIM BENNETT

MAKES: 3 large loaves

FROM MIXING TO OVEN: overnight
plus 9 hours, or twice overnight

BAKING TIME: 40–50 minutes

Jim originally created this loaf for the Dunblane Spring Fling in 2010. The idea was to include as many typically Scottish and locally produced ingredients as possible. It's a dark and dense bread, which emerges from the oven almost black thanks to its honey and egg wash.

FOR THE PRE-FERMENT:

400g/14oz/3⅓ cups wholemeal/
wholegrain spelt flour
240g/8½oz/1 cup water
70g/2½oz/5 tbsp rye sourdough
starter

FOR THE DOUGH:

600g/1lb 5oz/5 cups wholemeal/
wholegrain spelt flour
300g/10½oz/1¼ cups water
150g/5½oz/⅔ cup buttermilk
70g/2½oz/¾ cup barley flakes
70g/2½oz/¾ cup oat flakes
70g/2½oz/1 cup wheat bran
70g/2½oz/⅔ cup oat bran
50g/1¾oz/⅓ cup honey
50g/1¾oz/2½ tbsp barley malt extract
17g/3 tsp fine/table salt

FOR THE GLAZE:

1 egg
20g/1 generous tbsp honey

butter for greasing or flour for dusting

1. Mix the pre-ferment ingredients together, cover and leave at room temperature overnight.

2. Add the dough ingredients to the pre-ferment and mix thoroughly. Knead the dough until it is as smooth and stretchy as it can be, given the inclusion of flakes and bran. Return it to the bowl, cover and leave to prove at room temperature for about 4 hours, or overnight again in the refrigerator if this suits you better.

3. Grease three loaf tins or dust three proving baskets with flour. Divide the dough into 3 equal-size pieces, shape them to fit and place them seam-side down in tins, but seam-side up in baskets. Cover and leave to prove at room temperature for about 5 hours.

4. Heat the oven to 240°C/220°C fan/475°F/gas 8–9, with a baking stone or baking sheet in place if using baskets. Whisk the egg and honey together until thoroughly mixed. Brush this glaze over the tops of the loaves if in tins, then place them in the oven. If using baskets, turn the loaves out onto a floured peel, brush with glaze, and slide them onto the baking stone (it may be easier to do this one at a time).

5. Bake for 10 minutes, then turn the oven down to 190°C/170°C fan/375°F/gas 5 and continue to bake for a further 30–40 minutes. Keep an eye on the loaves, as the glaze is prone to burning. You might need to cover them loosely with foil before the baking time is up.

Sippet: Despite being created in the spring, the name of this loaf is Scots dialect for harvest or autumn bread.

Jim Bennett is, in his words, "a bald, portly, middle-aged Scotsman who loves his bread too much!" He's been baking Real Bread since being introduced to it by Andrew Whitley in 2008. He runs a pop-up microbakery in Dunblane, Scotland, baking for school and toddler group fundraisers.

Neil Baldwyn and Amy Burnage launched Lucky 13 in 2011, later renaming it No. Thirteen Craft Bakers. He says, "It was the perfect time to convince like-minded businesses in Birmingham to ditch the commercial stuff and start using Real Bread." The team and business continue to grow, on a mission to "work hard to build great relationships with our lovely customers, and to deliver the best bread we can".

Semolina Crown NEIL BALDWYN

As Britain's second city, it is surprising that Birmingham still only has a small handful of bakeries that have told us that they make what the Real Bread Campaign calls Real Bread. Neil and his partner Amy Burnage spotted this gap in the market back in 2011. This was one of the first breads Neil and Amy developed, and over their first few years he says it has remained a firm favourite among their Saturday specials.

MAKES: 1 loaf

FROM MIXING TO OVEN: 12–17 hours, or overnight plus 1–2 hours

BAKING TIME: 35 minutes

1. Mix all of the ingredients except the salt together thoroughly. Cover the dough and leave at room temperature for 45 minutes.

2. Add the salt and knead for a few minutes to incorporate it fully into the dough. Cover and leave to rest for 20 minutes.

3. Give the dough a single fold, cover and leave to rest for 20 minutes. Repeat this fold and rest process three more times.

4. Lightly flour the work surface and turn the dough out onto it, seam-side up. Shape it into a ball, cover and leave to rest for 30 minutes.

5. Shape the dough into a ball again, cover and leave to rest for 10 minutes. Poke a hole through the middle, then using both hands, gently and smoothly increase the size of the hole until it is about 10cm/4in in diameter and doesn't pull back. "Passing it through your hands like a rope works well for this", suggests Neil.

6. Place the dough seam-side up in a well-floured, ring-shaped proving basket, or seam-side down on a floured or oiled baking sheet, cover and leave to prove in the refrigerator for 8–12 hours (typically overnight).

7. Remove the dough from the refrigerator and leave for 1–2 hours to come up to ambient temperature. Meanwhile, heat the oven to 250°C/230°C fan/480°F/gas 9+, or as high as it will go, with a baking stone or baking sheet in place.

8. Turn the dough out of the proving basket, or slide it off the baking sheet, seam-side down onto a dusted peel. Slide the dough onto the baking stone, then immediately turn the oven down to 220°C/200°C fan/425°F/gas 7. Bake for 20 minutes, then turn the loaf around to ensure even baking, and continue to bake for a further 15 minutes. If the loaf looks too pale or dark, turn the temperature up or down by 10°C/20°F accordingly.

215g/7½oz/1½ cups white bread flour

150g/5½oz/2 cups fine semolina

65g/2¼oz/½ cup wholemeal/ wholegrain (dark) rye flour

280g/10oz/1¼ cups minus 1 tbsp water

85g/3oz/⅓ cup wheat or rye sourdough starter

45g/3 tbsp olive oil

8g/1½ tsp fine/table salt

Goats' Cheese and Honey Maslin

NICOLA WILLIS

MAKES: 1 loaf

FROM MIXING TO OVEN: overnight plus 6–8 hours

BAKING TIME: 35–40 minutes

Nicola said, "This loaf brings it all together: using time and the best local ingredients to make great Real Bread. The richness of the Welsh honey we use contrasts with the sharpness of the Ragstone cheese, all balanced by the light texture and gentle taste of the sourdough." Ragstone is an unpasteurized lactic goats' milk cheese, made in Herefordshire's Golden Valley, and you should look for an artisanal chevre or something similar when you make this loaf.

FOR THE PRE-FERMENT:

90g/3¼oz/6 tbsp rye sourdough starter

60g/2¼oz/¼ cup water

120g/4¼oz/¾ cup plus 2 tbsp white bread flour

FOR THE DOUGH:

270g/9½oz/scant 2 cups white bread flour

150g/5½oz/scant ⅔ cup water

60g/2¼oz/½ cup wholemeal/ wholegrain (dark) rye flour

20g/generous 1 tbsp honey

5g/1 tsp fine/table salt

80g/2¾oz/⅓ cup soft goats' cheese

20g/generous 1 tbsp honey, for drizzling

semolina or polenta/cornmeal, for dusting

1. Mix the pre-ferment ingredients together, cover and leave at room temperature overnight, or refrigerate overnight and bring it out 2 hours before needed.

2. Mix the pre-ferment and dough ingredients together, cover and leave to rest at room temperature for 10 minutes. Instead of kneading the dough, give it four separate single folds, with rests of 10–15 minutes after each fold, then leave the dough to prove for a further 1 hour.

3. Shape the dough carefully into a square about 1cm/½in thick. Break the cheese into pieces, distribute them evenly over the dough and gently press them in. Drizzle with honey.

4. Fold the 4 corners of the dough into the middle to cover the cheese, form the dough into a ball and seal the seams tightly.

5. Dust a proving basket well with semolina or polenta/cornmeal, shape the dough to fit and place it in, seam-side up. Cover and leave to prove for 4–6 hours at room temperature (alternatively, prove in the refrigerator overnight again, and remove 1 hour before baking).

6. Heat the oven to 240°C/220°C fan/475°F/gas 8–9, with a baking stone or baking sheet in place. Dust a peel with semolina or polenta/cornmeal, turn the dough out onto it and slash along the middle of the top with a sharp knife, or if you feel confident, slash a pattern into the dough. Slide the loaf onto the baking stone. Bake for 35–40 minutes until the crust is golden, or darker if you prefer.

Nicola **Willis** joined The Bakers' Table when it opened at the newly restored Talgarth Mill in Wales in 2011, and began baking professionally in 2012. The ethos of the business is to showcase high-quality, local ingredients and the café's menu is based around Real Bread baked using flour from the watermill. Nicola now runs monthly baking classes to share her skills with enthusiastic amateurs.

Hackney Wild Sourdough

BEN MACKINNON

Through the Real Bread Campaign, I've met quite a few people who have said "Sod this", quit their jobs, and become bakers. Ben MacKinnon is one of them. I first met Ben in the early days of his railway arch bakery, where he'd built an oven from salvaged materials. This is the basic recipe for the E5 Bakehouse's signature sourdough. It depends on long, slow fermentation to develop a robust dough with a deep, complex flavour.

MAKES: 1 large loaf
FROM MIXING TO OVEN: 3 days
BAKING TIME: 40 minutes

FOR THE PRE-FERMENT:
35g/1¼oz/2½ tbsp wheat or rye sourdough starter
30g/1oz/2 tbsp water
40g/1½oz/4½ tbsp white bread flour
12g/½oz/3½ heaping tsp wholemeal/ wholewheat bread flour

FOR THE FIRST-STAGE DOUGH:
85g/3oz/⅓ cup water
125g/4½oz/¾ cup plus 2 tbsp white bread flour
30g/1oz/scant 3½ tbsp wholemeal/ wholewheat bread flour

FOR THE FINAL DOUGH:
215g/7½oz/1 cup minus 2 tbsp water
245g/8½oz/1¾ cups white bread flour
45g/1½oz/5 tbsp wholemeal/ wholewheat bread flour
8g/1½ tsp fine/table salt

1. Mix the pre-ferment ingredients together thoroughly, cover and leave in the refrigerator for 6 hours.

2. Add the first-stage dough ingredients to the pre-ferment and mix together thoroughly. Cover and leave in the refrigerator to ferment for 2 days, or until active and bubbling.

3. Add all of the final dough ingredients, except the salt, to the first-stage dough and mix together thoroughly. Cover and leave to rest for 30 minutes.

4. Add the salt and knead for a few minutes to mix it in thoroughly. Cover the dough and leave at room temperature for 2½ hours, giving it a single fold every 30 minutes.

5. Shape the dough to fit a large proving basket, flour both dough and basket well and place the dough in the basket, seam-side up. Cover and leave to prove in the refrigerator for 12 hours (typically overnight).

6. Heat the oven to 250°C/230°C fan/480°F/gas 9+, or as high as it will go, with a baking stone or baking sheet in place. Turn the dough out onto a well-floured peel, slash the top and slide it onto the baking stone. Bake for 40 minutes, turning the loaf around after 20 minutes to ensure even baking.

Ben MacKinnon became a baker in 2009, starting E5 Bakehouse using a pizza restaurant's wood-fired oven and running a local home delivery round. In spring 2010, he built his own wood-fired rocket oven, fuelled by carpenters' offcuts, in a railway/railroad arch. E5 runs entirely on renewable energy, delivers all products by bicycle and continues to evolve, for example by setting up its own small flour mill on site.

Multigrain Pain au Levain

ROSS BAXTER

Levain is simply the French word for sourdough starter and *pain au levain* is bread made using it. Bread made with baker's yeast is *pain au levure*.

MAKES: 1 large loaf
FROM MIXING TO OVEN: 14–18 hours, or overnight plus 6 hours
BAKING TIME: 30–35 minutes

1. Mix the pre-ferment ingredients together, cover and leave at room temperature for 8–12 hours (typically overnight). Mix the soaker ingredients together in a separate bowl, cover and also leave at room temperature for 8–12 hours. Towards the end of that time, mix the dough flour and water together, cover and leave for a 1-hour autolyse.

2. Add the soaker and pre-ferment to the dough and mix thoroughly, then knead until the dough is smooth and stretchy. Cover and leave at room temperature for 3 hours.

3. Shape the dough into a ball, cover and leave to rise for 30 minutes.

4. Reshape the loaf, wet the top slightly and roll it in sunflower seeds. Place seam-side up in a large floured proving basket, cover and leave to prove for 2 hours.

5. Put a large casserole dish/Dutch oven or other heavy, ovenproof, lidded cooking pot in the oven and heat to 230°C/210°C fan/450°F/ gas 8. Using a heatproof cloth or oven gloves, lift the pot out onto a safe working area that the base of the pan won't scorch.

6. Carefully turn the dough seam-side down into the pot, slash the top of the dough, place the lid on, put it back in the oven and bake for 20 minutes. Remove the lid and continue to bake for a further 10–15 minutes.

FOR THE PRE-FERMENT:
50g/1¾oz/3½ tbsp white sourdough starter
30g/1oz/scant 3½ tbsp white bread flour
50g/1¾oz/heaping ⅓ cup wholemeal/ wholewheat bread flour
45g/1½oz/3 tbsp water

FOR THE SOAKER:
35g/1¼oz/¼ cup sunflower seeds
35g/1¼oz/¼ cup linseeds/flaxseeds
35g/1¼oz/¼ cup cracked rye
35g/1¼oz/⅓ cup rolled oats
8g/1½ tsp fine/table salt
65g/2¼oz/scant ½ cup wholemeal/ wholewheat bread flour
185g/6½oz/¾ cup water

FOR THE DOUGH:
265g/9¼oz/scant 2 cups wholemeal/ wholewheat bread flour
165g/5¾oz/¾ cup minus 1 tbsp water

sunflower seeds, for topping

Ross Baxter's surname has its roots in the Old English for baker and he comes from a family of them. In 2011, he became head baker of the community-owned co-operative Bakery Dunbar. Since spring 2014 he has led the team at Bostock Bakery in North Berwick. He says, "We are extremely passionate about everything we do and one thing we do really well is bake bread, Real Bread; bread that comforts you and gives you a big hug; bread that just tastes really damn good!"

Sungmo Kim started to learn to bake while at university. Later, while enjoying baking Real Bread for his family, he pictured that this could become his job. He bought a small oven and in April 2015 converted a space at his home in Daegu, South Korea, to launch Loaf and Salt Bakehouse microbakery.

Millet Porridge and Wheat Loaf

SUNGMO KIM

Millet is an important food crop, notably in south and east Asia and sub-Saharan Africa. In Korea, it is often made into a porridge, and that's how it is used in this recipe. Don't confuse the whole anise seeds used here (from the herbaceous annual *Pimpinella anisum*) with the star anise used in Chinese and Indian cooking.

MAKES: 1 loaf

FROM MIXING TO OVEN: 3 days

BAKING TIME: 35–40 minutes

1. Mix the pre-ferment ingredients together, cover and leave at room temperature for about 16–18 hours (typically until the next day) until bubbly.

2. Put the millet and water into a pan, bring to the boil, then reduce the heat, cover and simmer until the water has been absorbed by the millet. Leave the porridge to cool and refrigerate until needed.

3. Mix the pre-ferment with the water and both flours from the dough recipe. Cover and prove in the refrigerator for a further 24 hours.

4. Mix the salt into the dough until fully incorporated. Cover and leave to rest at room temperature for 20 minutes. Give the dough a single fold, cover and leave to rest for another 20 minutes.

5. Add the millet porridge and remaining dough ingredients and mix thoroughly. Cover and leave to rest for 20 minutes.

6. Give the dough another single fold, rest it for 20 minutes, give it one final single fold, then cover and leave the dough to rise at room temperature for 4–5 hours.

7. Grease a large loaf tin, shape the dough to fit and place seam-side down in the tin. Dust the top of the dough with flour, cover and leave to prove in the refrigerator for 12–16 hours (typically until the next day.)

8. Take the dough out of the refrigerator 1–2 hours before baking. Heat the oven to 240°C/220°C fan/475°F/gas 8–9 and bake the loaf for 35–40 minutes, checking after about 15 minutes that it isn't browning too quickly: turn the oven down to 220°C/200°C fan/425°F/gas 7 if it is.

FOR THE PRE-FERMENT:

45g/1½oz/5 tbsp brown bread flour (or half white, half wholemeal/wholewheat)

45g/1½oz/3 tbsp water

5g/1 tsp wholemeal/wholewheat sourdough starter

FOR THE MILLET PORRIDGE:

45g/1½oz/¼ cup millet

85g/3oz/⅓ cup water

FOR THE DOUGH:

180g/6¼oz/¾ cup water

85g/3oz/½ cup plus 1 tbsp brown bread flour (or half white, half wholemeal/wholewheat)

135g/4¾oz/scant 1 cup wholemeal/wholewheat bread flour

4g/¾ tsp fine/table salt

5g/1 tsp chia seeds

30g/1 oz/scant ¼ cup dried cherries

2–3g/½–¾ tsp anise seeds

15g/½oz/2 tbsp sesame seeds

butter or oil, for greasing

Apple Sourdough ROB TAYLOR

MAKES: 2 loaves

FROM MIXING TO OVEN: 5–7 hours, or overnight plus 2 hours

BAKING TIME: 25–30 minutes

Rob tells us that this recipe was originally created by Matthew McCarthy, who was his mentor when he first joined The Welbeck Bakehouse team. Since then, it has remained a firm favourite for staff and customers alike. It makes an incredible bacon sandwich and cheese on toast to die for.

200g/7oz/2 cups unpeeled, cored and thinly sliced dessert apple, for drying

200g/7oz/2 cups unpeeled, cored and diced dessert apple, for cooking

12g/5 tsp ground mixed spice/ pumpkin pie spice

300g/10½oz/2 cups plus 2 tbsp strong white bread flour

40g/1½oz/⅓ cup wholemeal/ wholegrain (dark) rye flour

40g/1½oz/scant ⅓ cup wholemeal/ wholewheat bread flour

270g/9½oz/1 cup plus 2 tbsp hand-warm water

115g/4oz/scant ½ cup white sourdough starter

8g/1½ tsp fine/table salt

butter or oil, for greasing

1. Lay the sliced apple on a baking sheet lined with non-stick baking parchment and bake at 140–150°C/120–130°C fan/275–300°F/gas 1–2 until 80–90% dehydrated: dry but not crispy. Separately, cook the diced apple in a pan until soft but not mushy. Leave both to cool, then measure 75g/2½oz/scant 1 cup dried apple and 150g/5½oz/ 1 cup cooked apple into a bowl and fold in the mixed spice/pumpkin pie spice.

2. Put all three flours into a large bowl, add the water and mix together thoroughly until no lumps or dry patches remain. Cover and leave for 1 hour, then add the sourdough starter and salt and knead for 5–7 minutes or until the dough is fully and evenly mixed together.

3. Add the apple/spice mixture and knead that into the dough as well. If the dough appears to be too dry or too wet, add a little water or flour to adjust this, and knead it in. Place the dough in a lightly greased bowl, at least 50% larger than the dough itself. Cover and leave to rise in a warm draught-free place for 2½–3 hours, giving the dough a single turn every 50–60 minutes.

4. Divide the dough into 2 equal-size pieces and shape them into balls. Place seam-side down on baking sheets dusted with a little flour, or seam-side up in floured proving baskets. Cover and leave to rise by 40–50% at room temperature, or more slowly in the refrigerator overnight, taking them out 1–2 hours before baking.

5. Heat oven to 230–240°C/210–220°C fan/450–475°F/gas 8–9. If you are using proving baskets, have a baking stone in place in the oven, and when ready to bake, turn the dough out onto a floured peel, slash the top of the dough and slide it carefully onto the stone. It may be easier to do this one loaf at a time. If using baking sheets, simply slash the dough before transferring to the oven on the baking sheets. Bake for 25–30 minutes.

Rob Taylor was a pastry chef and keen amateur baker before joining The Welbeck Bakehouse in 2013. With a passion for sourdough and viennoiserie and an eagerness to learn, Rob became head baker in 2014 and is supported by an incredibly hard-working and passionate team.

Buttermilk Rolls MATTHEW ROBERTS

MAKES: 12 rolls

FROM MIXING TO OVEN: overnight
plus 4–5 hours

BAKING TIME: 15 minutes

Matthew tells me that buttermilk was a mainstay of traditional Scottish baking, and that one of its effects is that it helps to soften the crumb of the bread. Once made from the fermented whey left over at the end of butter making, it's now usually produced by inoculating skimmed milk with a culture of lactic acid bacteria.

FOR THE PRE-FERMENT:

60g/2¼oz/¼ cup rye sourdough
starter
130g/4½oz/½ cup plus 2 tsp water
130g/4½oz/scant 1¼ cups wholemeal/
wholegrain (dark) rye flour

FOR THE DOUGH:

325g/11½oz/2⅓ cups wholemeal/
wholewheat bread flour
325g/11½oz/scant 2½ cups plain/
all-purpose flour
325g/11½oz/1⅓ cups water
170g/6oz/scant ¾ cup buttermilk
20g/1½ tbsp butter, plus extra
for greasing
15g/3 tsp fine/table salt

1.   Mix the pre-ferment ingredients together, cover and leave at room temperature overnight.

2.   The next day, mix the flours, water and buttermilk for the dough together thoroughly. Cover and leave to rest for 20 minutes.

3.   Warm the butter until it is barely melted, then mix it into the dough with the salt and the pre-ferment and knead for 5 minutes. Cover and leave to rest for 10 minutes. Knead the dough for another 5 minutes, rest again for 10 minutes, then give it one more 5-minute knead. You should have a smooth, stretchy dough. Cover and leave to rest for another 20 minutes.

4.   Give the dough a single fold, cover and leave to rest for 20 minutes, then repeat this fold and 20-minute rest.

5.   Grease a baking sheet with butter. Divide the dough into 12 equal-size pieces and shape them into balls. Place on the sheet about 5cm/2in apart, leaving room for them to grow (or closer, if you want to bake "batch" rolls that gently join together). Dust the tops with flour, cover and leave to prove at room temperature for 2 hours.

6.   Heat the oven to 250°C/230°C fan/480°F/gas 9+, or as high as it will go. Put the rolls into the oven on the baking sheet, immediately turn the oven down to 220°C/200°C fan/425°F/gas 7 and bake for around 15 minutes until golden brown.

Matthew Roberts began to bake for himself and his family when the only Real Bread baker in the area stopped selling through his local market. After Matthew and his wife Zillah moved to Scotland, a regular order from a nearby deli encouraged the couple to begin expanding their bakery, and so began the Steamie Bakehouse. In September 2013, the couple relocated to Yorkshire, where Matthew joined the team at Seven Hills Bakery.

Potato, Rosemary and Cracked Pepper Focaccia MARK WOODS

The Latin for "hearth" is *focus*, where a whole family of flattish breads including *focaccia* and *fougasse* were once baked, and from which they take their names. If you have a wood-fired pizza oven, this is one to try in it. Or like me, you can bake in a regular domestic oven.

MAKES: 1 loaf
FROM MIXING TO OVEN: 3½–6 hours
BAKING TIME: 15–20 minutes

1. Mix all of the dough ingredients together thoroughly. Cover and leave to rest for 10–15 minutes.

2. Knead the dough until smooth and stretchy. Cover and leave to prove at room temperature for 1–2 hours.

3. Meanwhile, cook the potatoes and sprig of rosemary in a pan of boiling water for 10–15 minutes until the potatoes are just soft. Drain, leave to cool and cut each potato in half, discarding the rosemary.

4. Grease a large baking sheet (flat or with sides up to 3cm/1¼in high) lightly with olive oil.

5. Turn the dough out onto a lightly floured or oiled work surface and shape into a rectangle about 2cm/¾in thick, to fit the baking sheet. You may find it easier to do this in two stages, leaving the dough to relax for 5–10 minutes in between.

6. Place the dough on the baking sheet and brush lightly with olive oil. Cover and leave to prove at room temperature for 2–3 hours.

7. Heat the oven to 230°C/210°C fan/450°F/gas 8. Push the potato pieces cut-side down into the dough, jab small holes into the dough and push in the rosemary leaves, then sprinkle with salt flakes and black pepper. Bake for 15–20 minutes, or until light golden brown. Serve when just cool.

FOR THE DOUGH:

50g/1¾oz/3½ tbsp white sourdough starter

150g/5½oz/about 1 cup white bread flour

150g/5½oz/1 cup plus 2 tbsp tipo 00 bread flour

150g/5½oz/scant ⅔ cup water

50g/1¾oz/3½ tbsp olive oil, plus a little extra for greasing and brushing

FOR THE TOPPING:

300g/10½oz/2⅓ cups baby new potatoes

5cm/2in sprig of rosemary

15–20 pairs of rosemary leaves

coarse sea salt flakes

freshly ground black pepper

Appam CHRIS YOUNG

This is a breakfast staple in southern India, traditionally made using the palm sap known locally as toddy, and left to ferment overnight. They are cooked in a shallow, concave pan called an *appachatti*, but you can use a frying pan, skillet or heavy wok. Make the rice sourdough starter in exactly the same way as a white sourdough starter (see page 14), using brown rice flour for at least the first one or two days. After that you can use white rice flour.

MAKES: 5–10, depending on size
FROM MIXING TO COOKING: overnight plus a few minutes
COOKING TIME: 2–4 minutes each

500g/1lb 2oz/2¾ cups white long grain rice

250g/9oz/generous 1 cup thick coconut milk

50g/1¾oz/3½ tbsp rice sourdough starter

15g/½oz/1 tbsp grated jaggery or soft dark brown sugar

5g/1 tsp fine/table salt

coconut or vegetable oil, for frying

1. Soak half the rice in water for 4–5 hours before draining it thoroughly. Meanwhile, cook the remaining rice in a pan of boiling water for about 15 minutes until soft, then drain that as well.

2. Grind both batches of rice with the coconut milk in a mortar and pestle, food blender or processor to make a smooth paste. Leave to cool slightly, then add the sourdough starter and continue to purée for about 5 minutes or until you have a thick, smooth batter. Cover and leave to ferment at room temperature overnight until it is bubbling, or even seething.

3. Add the jaggery and salt to the batter and mix well.

4. Lightly oil an appachatti and warm over a medium heat for a few minutes. Pour in a ladleful of batter, swirl it around to make a circle about 15cm/6in in diameter and 5mm/¼in thick at the middle and cook for a few minutes until it is set and cooked through. The idea is to have it thick in the middle and very thin at the edges, which gives it a spongy centre and a lacy, lightly browned crispy fringe. Remove with heatproof tongs and repeat with the remaining batter until it is all used up.

Baker's Tip As an alternative to coconut milk, use equal weights of water and fresh or desiccated/dried shredded coconut.

Sourdough Pitta JACK SMYLIE WILD

Pitta shares its heritage, and etymology, with pizza, pide and other low-risen breads found from eastern Europe to the Levant. To create the "pocket" that pitta is known for, a really good thwack of bottom heat is essential, from an oven with a stone floor or a really hot baking stone in it. With that, the oven spring in such a thin dough will push it to form a single bubble. Jack says, "Stuff them with falafel, slaw, hummus, harissa, minty yogurt and grilled halloumi."

MAKES: 6 pittas
FROM MIXING TO OVEN: 5½–7 hours
BAKING TIME: 2–4 minutes each batch

1. Mix the flour, water and sourdough starter together thoroughly. Cover and leave at room temperature for 1 hour.

2. Stretch the dough out, sprinkle the salt over it and work it in for a few minutes to make sure it's evenly distributed and starting to dissolve. Knead the dough for 5–10 minutes, then cover and leave to prove at room temperature for 3–4 hours until pillowy.

3. Dust the work surface with semolina or flour. Divide the dough into 6 equal-size pieces, shape them into balls, place on the dusted work surface, cover and leave to prove for 40–60 minutes.

4. Heat the oven to 250°C/230°C fan/480°F/gas 9+, or as high as it will go, with a baking stone or baking sheet in place. Roll out each ball of dough to an oval about 5mm/¼in thick. Cover and leave to rest for 5–10 minutes.

5. Using a floured peel, slide as many of the pittas as will fit onto the hot baking stone. Bake for 2–4 minutes until puffed up, without letting them brown or crisp. Wrap in a clean dish towel while cooling so that the escaping steam stays close to the pittas and helps to keep them supple, while you bake the remaining pieces of dough.

315g/11oz/2¼ cups white bread flour
210g/7½oz/1 cup minus 2 tbsp water
70g/2½oz/5 tbsp wholemeal/ wholewheat sourdough starter
5g/1 tsp fine/table salt
semolina, for dusting (optional)

Jack Smylie Wild is a self-taught sourdough fanatic. Having grown up in Devon, he returned to his native Wales, where he soon became frustrated by the lack of Real Bread on offer. Always a keen cook, he decided to take matters into his own hands and set up his bakehouse café Bara Menyn (literally "bread and butter") in Cardigan in February 2015. He says his meticulous approach to the sourdough process quickly gained a loyal following of Real Breadheads.

Sourdough Pizza Margherita

OTTAVIA MAZZONI

MAKES: 4 thin pizzas
FROM MIXING TO OVEN: 9–11 hours
BAKING TIME: 4–5 minutes each

I met Ottavia on the course at Schumacher College that first led me to the Real Bread Campaign. She says that this recipe is the result of years of attempts at making a good sourdough pizza suitable for baking in a domestic oven. She reckons that this one is the best yet.

FOR THE DOUGH:

150g/5½oz/⅔ cup white sourdough
   starter
250g/9oz/1 cup plus 1 tbsp water
350g/12oz/2⅔ cups plain/
   all-purpose flour
50g/1¾oz/¼ cup fine durum wheat
   semolina
5g/1 tsp fine/table salt
15g/1 tbsp olive oil

FOR THE TOPPING:

125g/4½oz mozzarella
400g/14oz/1¾ cups canned chopped
   tomatoes
a generous pinch of dried oregano
olive oil, to taste
salt and freshly ground black pepper
a handful of basil leaves

1. Mix the starter with 200g/7oz/¾ cup of the water and 250g/9oz/ scant 2 cups of the flour. Cover and leave at room temperature for about 4 hours.

2. Add in half of the remaining water, the rest of the flour and the semolina, salt and olive oil and mix thoroughly. Cover and leave to rest for 10 minutes. If the dough is feeling tight (it should be quite soft and stretchy) add in more of the water. Knead the dough until it loses its stickiness and becomes smooth and elastic. Shape into a ball, cover and leave to prove at room temperature for 2–3 hours.

3. Divide the dough into 4 equal-size pieces, shape into balls. Place these on a work surface or baking sheet dusted with semolina, cover and leave to prove for another 2–3 hours.

4. If you have a pizza oven, fire it up! Otherwise, place a baking stone on the top shelf of the oven and heat it up, as hot as it will get: 250°C/230°C fan/480°F/gas 9+. Meanwhile, drain the mozzarella, slice it thinly and pat off any excess liquid with paper towels. Pour the chopped tomatoes with their juices into a bowl and season with oregano, olive oil, salt and pepper to taste.

5. Flatten each ball of dough on a floured work surface, patting it down with your hands, starting from the middle and letting the dough spread gently, leaving a slightly risen border around the edge. You might need to do this in two stages with a 5-minute rest in between.

6. Transfer 1 base onto a well-floured peel. Top with tomatoes followed by slices of mozzarella, then drizzle with olive oil. Slide the pizza onto the baking stone, trying not to disturb the filling. Bake until done, which hopefully won't take more than about 4–5 minutes, so keep an eye on it. Repeat with the remaining pizza bases. Serve with a scattering of basil leaves and a twist of pepper.

Ottavia Mazzoni is an Italian home baker and cookery teacher based near Bath in the west of England, where she moved in 2001. A keen cook and baker since childhood, in 2010 she set up Ottavia in Cucina cookery and baking school to share her passion for good, uncomplicated food and Real Bread. She also founded the Box Community Sourdough Project, a not-for-profit skill share scheme based in the village of Box, on a mission to teach as many people as possible how to make genuine sourdough bread.

Sourdough Pretzels URSI WIDEMANN

Ursi says, "I love pretzels! I could eat them every single day . . . maybe it's because I'm Bavarian". Pretzels are usually dipped in a solution of sodium hydroxide (lye) prior to baking, which gives them their characteristic taste and shiny brown skin. As food-grade sodium hydroxide can be hard to obtain and is hazardous to handle, this recipe uses bicarbonate of soda/baking soda instead, which gets you safely toward a similar result.

MAKES: 12

FROM MIXING TO OVEN: 12–16 hours

BAKING TIME: 15–20 minutes

FOR THE PRE-FERMENT:

125g/4½oz/¾ cup plus 2 tbsp
   wholemeal/wholewheat bread flour
20g/1½ tbsp rye sourdough starter
100g/3½oz/½ cup minus 1 tbsp water

FOR THE DOUGH:

375g/13oz/2⅔ cups white bread flour
25g/1oz/2 tbsp butter
8g/1½ tsp fine/table salt
160g/5¾oz/⅔ cup water

FOR DIPPING:

1kg/2lb 4oz/4¼ cups water
20g/heaping 1½ tbsp bicarbonate
   of soda/baking soda

FOR THE TOPPING:

coarse sea salt flakes or crystals,
   or you could use sesame seeds,
   poppy seeds or caraway seeds

1. Mix the pre-ferment ingredients together, cover and leave at room temperature for 8–12 hours until bubbly.

2. Mix the dough ingredients with the pre-ferment, and knead until you have a firm but supple dough: tighter than usual, but if it really is too stiff to work, add a little more water. Put the dough into a bowl, cover and leave to rise at room temperature for a further 3 hours, giving the dough a single fold halfway through this time.

3. Divide the dough into 12 equal-size pieces (65g/2¼oz), roll into balls, cover and leave for 20 minutes, then roll each piece into a strand about 25cm/10in long that tapers at the ends with a little belly in the middle. Bend each strand into a "U" shape, cross one side over the other about halfway up (fig. 1), give it a twist where they cross (fig. 2), then fold the ends up to meet the bend of the U and press down gently to fix in place (fig. 3). Cover the dough and leave to prove for 45–60 minutes.

4. Line a baking sheet with non-stick baking parchment and heat the oven to 230°C/210°C fan/450°F/gas 8. Meanwhile, bring the water to the boil in a large pan and add the bicarbonate of soda/baking soda. Drop the pretzels into the boiling liquid 2 or 3 at a time for 20 seconds, lift out with a slotted spoon and place onto the baking sheet. Immediately sprinkle with the topping of your choice while the dough is still tacky. Slash the dough at its fattest part and bake for 15–20 minutes until deep brown.

Ursi Widemann set up The Little Bear microbakery in the kitchen of her London home. Originally from Germany, her Real Bread adventures have included a Bread Angels course and stints at Baker and Spice in Dubai and the Biohotel Kurz in Berchtesgaden, Germany.

Crumpets PETER COOK

MAKES: up to 20, depending on size
FROM MIXING TO COOKING: overnight plus 3–4 hours
COOKING TIME: 8–9 minutes per batch

Real crumpets are amazing! Used instead of an English muffin as the foundation of eggs Benedict, or simply toasted and spread liberally with butter that melts and dribbles down your fingers and served with a steaming mug of tea, they are "the business". Peter created this recipe while he was head baker at S.C. Price in Ludlow, inspired by one used in the 1940s by the bakery's founder Sid Price.

200g/7oz/1½ cups minus 1 tbsp white bread flour

200g/7oz/1½ cups plain/all-purpose flour

200g/7oz/¾ cup plus 1 tbsp white sourdough starter

200g/7oz/¾ cup plus 1 tbsp milk

200g/7oz/¾ cup plus 1 tbsp water

10g/2 tsp fine/table salt

10g/2 tsp vegetable oil

5g/1 tsp caster/superfine sugar

5g/1 tsp fresh yeast

110g/3¾oz/scant ½ cup sparkling water

butter or oil, for greasing

1. Mix all of the ingredients together, except the sparkling water, cover and leave in the refrigerator overnight.

2. Remove the bowl from the refrigerator, stir the batter, cover and leave at room temperature for 3–4 hours, or until many bubbles appear on the surface.

3. Lightly grease a griddle or heavy frying pan and as many 8.5cm/3¼in crumpet rings as will fit onto it. Place over a medium-high heat.

4. Stir the sparkling water into the batter and ladle some of the batter into each ring to a depth of no more than 1cm/½in.

5. Cook each crumpet for 6–7 minutes until bubbles rise to the surface and burst to leave holes and the batter has set. The trick is to get the temperature hot enough to set the crumpets before the holes start to collapse, but not so hot that their bottoms burn before they are cooked throughout (you may want to cook one "test crumpet" before going for a pan full!).

6. Remove the rings, flip the crumpets over and cook for a few minutes more until they are lightly browned. Re-grease the rings before cooking the next batch.

Sippet: Etymologists can't agree on the origin of the word crumpet. Theories include it coming from the Welsh *crempog* or Breton *krampouz*, or possibly having the same Germanic root as crumple.

Peter Cook began baking in 1991 at S.C. Price & Sons in Ludlow, Shropshire, where he helped the bakery to win national plaudits, including from Waitrose, the World Bread Awards and Baking Industry Awards. In 2014 Peter moved to Ledbury and started Peter Cooks Bread with Bread Angel, Shona Kelly. The wholesale bakery supplies businesses in Herefordshire and Worcestershire and in 2014 were the overall winners of the World Bread Awards for their ciabatta.

Chestnut Muffins SIMON POFFLEY

Simon originally created these chestnut flour English muffins when he was a member of a now-disbanded bakers' collective, which ran a fortnightly stall at a farmers' market in Stoke Newington, east London. He says that they always used to "stash some away for a post-market toasting, spread with chestnut purée if possible!"

MAKES: 12 English muffins
FROM MIXING TO COOKING: overnight plus 2–3 hours
COOKING TIME: 15 minutes per batch

1. Mix all of the dough ingredients together thoroughly. Cover and leave to rest at room temperature for 15 minutes, then knead for about 10 minutes. Cover and leave to prove for 1 hour, then give the dough a single fold. Cover and leave to prove in the refrigerator overnight (12–14 hours).

2. Remove the dough from the refrigerator about 2–3 hours before baking. After 1 hour, give the dough a double fold, then leave it to relax for at least 15 minutes. Dust the work surface with rice flour or semolina and roll the dough out to about 1cm/½in thick. Cut the dough into circles using an 8.5cm/3¼in cookie cutter or a crumpet/ poached egg ring. Dust excess flour from the offcuts and press them together, leaving the dough to rest again before rolling out and cutting more muffins, until it is all used up.

3. Dust the unbaked muffins with more rice flour or semolina, cover and leave to prove at room temperature for 1 hour. Heat a griddle or heavy frying pan over a medium-high heat. Place 3 or 4 muffins in the pan and cook for about 10 minutes, lifting with a spatula every few minutes to check that they are not over-browning. Flip them over and cook for about another 5 minutes until browned on both sides. Place on a wire cooling rack. When cool, the muffins can be split, toasted and buttered.

115g/4oz/scant ½ cup white sourdough starter
300g/10½oz/scant 1½ cups plain yogurt
170g/6oz/scant ¾ cup water
225g/8oz/2½ cups chestnut flour
500g/1lb 2oz/3½ cups white bread flour (or about 550g/1lb 4oz/ 4 cups wholemeal/wholewheat bread flour)
10g/2 tsp fine/table salt
rice flour or semolina, for dusting

Simon Poffley started baking sourdough loaves to recreate the breads he'd eaten in Russia, Poland and Germany. From 2010 to 2013, he was part of the Hornbeam Bakers' Collective, before moving on to found The Fermentarium, home to sourdough classes, pizza baking in a cob oven and the Left Bank Brewery, as part of delving into other fermentation techniques.

Wayne Caddy is Head of Baking at the School of Artisan Food and owner of The Essential Baker. Having trained at Sheffield and Leeds colleges, he was awarded Student Baker of the Year. Over more than 20 years, he has baked all over the world, sharing his knowledge of all things Real Bread. Wayne has represented the UK at the baking Coupe du Monde, and more recently was the first baker from the UK to compete in the prestigious Masters de la Boulangerie; only a handful of the top bakers from around the world are selected.

Bara Brith WAYNE CADDY

Bara brith is Welsh for "speckled bread", and as with so many recipes from around the world, there are probably nearly as many versions as there are towns and villages or even families in its homeland. Wayne has eschewed the baker's yeast often used and says that "the sourdough provides a subtle flavour, which works to complement the other ingredients". He adds, "packed with fruit and lightly spiced, this iconic Welsh tea loaf is best served with delicious real butter".

MAKES: 2 small loaves
FROM MIXING TO OVEN: 6½–10½ hours
BAKING TIME: 45 minutes

1. For this recipe, you need to create a sourdough starter at 60% hydration: 3 parts water (by weight) to every 5 parts flour (e.g. 75g/3oz/ 5 tbsp water to every 125g/5oz/¾ cup plus 2 tbsp flour). You can do this from day one, or adapt an existing starter with several refreshments in this ratio.

2. Mix the pre-ferment ingredients together. Cover and leave in a warm place (35–40°C/95–105°F) for 2–3 hours, or longer in a cooler place, until it becomes puffy.

3. Add the milk, flour and salt to the pre-ferment, mix thoroughly and knead until you have a smooth, stretchy dough, then add the sugar, lard and butter to the dough and continue kneading until they are worked into the dough and it is smooth and silky again.

4. Mix together the dried fruits and spice. Flatten the dough into a rectangle, scatter the fruit over it and work it into the dough until distributed evenly, taking care not to mash the fruit up. Shape the dough into a ball, cover and leave to prove in a warm place (about 30°C/85°F) for 1 hour.

5. Give the dough a single fold, cover and leave to continue proving for a further 2–3 hours.

6. Grease two 500g/1lb loaf tins, divide the dough into 2 equal-size pieces, shape them to fit and place in the tins, seam-side down. Cover and leave somewhere warm (20–30°C/70–85°F) for 1–3 hours until doubled in size.

7. Heat the oven to 190°C/170°C fan/375°F/gas 5. Bake the loaves for 45 minutes, then remove them from the oven and turn them out of the tins onto a wire cooling rack. Leave to cool for 10–15 minutes and brush the tops with the apricot glaze while still warm.

FOR THE PRE-FERMENT:

50g/1¾oz/heaping ⅓ cup wholemeal/ wholewheat bread flour

50g/1¾oz/heaping ⅓ cup white bread flour

65g/2¼oz/¼ cup whole milk

100g/3½oz/scant ½ cup firm white sourdough starter (60% hydration)

FOR THE DOUGH:

240g/8½oz/1 cup whole milk

240g/8½oz/about 1¾ cups white bread flour

5g/1 tsp fine/table salt

60g/2¼oz/scant ⅓ cup packed soft brown sugar

35g/1¼oz/2 tbsp lard

35g/1¼oz/2 tbsp butter, plus extra for greasing

230g/8oz/1¾ cups currants

100g/3½oz/½ cup sultanas/golden raisins

30g/1oz/scant ¼ cup mixed peel/ candied peel

3g/½ tsp ground mixed spice/pumpkin pie spice

FOR THE GLAZE:

1–2 tbsp apricot jam, diluted with a little boiling water

Waterloo Buns JOHN TOWNSHEND

While bearing a strong family resemblance to their older Chelsea bun cousins, what John has created here is instead leavened with sourdough starter; leaves out the often used milk, eggs and lemon peel; and uses marmalade and cream as a glaze, with the spices there, rather than in the dough. As with many of John's creations, these are named after a battle, as he says, "Each loaf is a small victory for life, crafted with nature rather than against it."

MAKES: 12 buns
FROM MIXING TO OVEN: 8½–13½ hours
BAKING TIME: 25 minutes

FOR THE PRE-FERMENT:

75g/2¾oz/5 tbsp white sourdough starter at 75% hydration

130g/4½oz/1 cup minus 1 tbsp white bread flour

100g/3½oz/¾ cup minus 1 tbsp wholemeal/wholewheat bread flour

25g/1oz/scant ¼ cup wholemeal/ wholegrain (dark) rye flour

190g/6¾oz/¾ cup plus 1 tbsp water

FOR THE DOUGH:

300g/10½oz/2 cups plus 2 tbsp white bread flour

100g/3½oz/½ cup minus 1 tbsp water

55g/2oz/⅓ cup caster/superfine sugar

6g/1 tsp fine/table salt

70g/2½oz/5 tbsp unsalted butter

FOR THE FILLING AND GLAZE:

100g/3½oz/¾ cup raisins

a little water and brandy

40g/1½oz/3 tbsp unsalted butter, softened, plus extra for greasing

30g/1oz/2 tbsp caster/superfine sugar

50g/1¾oz/scant ¼ cup marmalade

2–3g/about ¾ tsp ground mixed spice/pumpkin pie spice

25g/1oz/2 tbsp double/heavy cream

1. For this recipe, you need a sourdough starter at 75% hydration: a flour to water ratio of 4:3 by weight, or 100g/4oz/¾ cup minus 1 tbsp flour to every 75g/3oz/scant ⅓ cup of water. The day before baking, cover the raisins for the filling with a mixture of water and brandy, and leave to soak.

2. The next day, mix all of the pre-ferment ingredients together thoroughly, cover and leave at room temperature for 4–8 hours, then mix the pre-ferment with all of the dough ingredients except the butter. Knead the dough until smooth, then knead in the butter until fully absorbed and the dough is smooth and silky again. Cover the dough and leave at room temperature for 2 hours, giving it a single fold after 40 minutes.

3. Dust the work surface and a rolling pin with flour and roll out the dough to a rectangle about 30x36cm/12x14in and 5mm/¼in thick. Cover the dough and leave it to rest for 5–10 minutes, then beat the butter and sugar for the filling together and spread this evenly over the dough. Drain the raisins and dot them evenly over the dough. Roll up the dough from a short edge like a Swiss/jelly roll, then dust the outside with flour. Cut this into 12 equal-size slices.

4. Grease a 30x25cm/12x10in baking tin with sides at least 5cm/2in high, and arrange the dough slices, lying flat and about 1cm/½in apart. Cover and leave to prove at room temperature for 2–3 hours until they are touching and about 5cm/2in high.

5. Heat the oven to 180°C/160°C fan/350°F/gas 4 and bake the buns for about 25 minutes until golden brown. Meanwhile, warm the marmalade in a pan over a low heat until just liquid, then add the spice, remove from the heat and stir in the cream. Transfer the buns from the oven onto a wire rack and leave to cool for 5–10 minutes, then drizzle the glaze over them.

John Townshend has always loved good bread, but didn't discover what it really meant until he moved to Munich. A decade later, on returning to London, he started to bake his own sourdough loaves. Recognizing not just the need for a local bakery, but the role it and Real Bread could play in his south London community, John created the Kennington Bakery in March 2015.

Jennine Walker and Claudia Ehmke have been baking together in their home in Hackney, London, for the past three years, making it up as they go along, with a bit of help from a course at the E5 Bakehouse and a lot of inspiration from travelling and foraging. They love taking their loaves out for a walk and picnic in the countryside, as well as sharing them with friends and family.

Double Chocolate Sourdough

JENNINE WALKER

Jennine told me that this recipe was inspired by a chocolate baguette she found in a Boulogne-sur-Mer bakery one rainy spring day on a weekend trip to France. After several attempts to recreate this at home, she came up with this recipe, which she says is pretty close to how she remembers the flavour, if not the texture.

MAKES: 1 large loaf

FROM MIXING TO OVEN: overnight plus 3–4 hours

BAKING TIME: 35–45 minutes

1. Mix the sourdough starter, flour and water together thoroughly, cover and leave at room temperature for 12 hours (typically overnight).

2. Add the cocoa powder, honey and salt and mix well. Cover and leave to rest for 10 minutes.

3. Knead the dough for around 10–15 seconds, cover and leave to rest for 10–15 minutes. Repeat this knead/rest process until you have a smooth, stretchy, silky dough.

4. Add the chocolate chips and work the dough until they are evenly distributed. Cover and leave the dough to prove for 1 hour, giving it a fold after 30 minutes.

5. Dust a proving basket well with flour. Shape the dough to fit, and put it in the basket, seam-side up. Cover and leave to prove at room temperature for 1–2 hours until doubled in size and the dough doesn't spring back when pressed gently.

6. Heat the oven to 250°C/230°C fan/480°F/gas 9+, or as high as it will go, with a baking stone or baking sheet in place. Tip the dough out onto a well-floured peel, slash the top and slide it onto the baking stone. Turn the oven down immediately to 200°C/180°C fan/400°F/gas 6 and bake for 35–45 minutes, turning the loaf round in the oven after 15 minutes to ensure even baking, and cover the top with a sheet of kitchen foil if it is browning too quickly.

300g/10½oz/1¼ cups white sourdough starter
200g/7oz/1½ cups minus 1 tbsp white bread flour
160g/5¾oz/⅔ cup water
40g/1½oz/scant ½ cup cocoa powder
15g/1 tbsp honey
6g/1 tsp fine/table salt
100g/3½oz/about ⅔ cup dark/bittersweet chocolate chips

Leftovers

Food is too precious to waste; a truth that can be forgotten when so much is sold relatively (and even unrealistically) cheaply, but less so when you have paid an honest price or crafted it yourself.

"Wasting Real Bread? Who does that?", you might ask, but these things happen, even to those of us who try our darnedest to avoid it.

There are several ways of reducing bread waste, including double checking with yourself (and your bread bin) how much you really need to buy or bake; choosing to make genuine sourdough (the process has a natural preservative effect); using a wetter dough, which slows staling; not putting bread in the refrigerator, which speeds staling; and slicing a loaf to freeze so you can keep it for when it's needed.

If all of these fail, this section contains a handful of ideas for what to do with the crusts, crumbs and chunks of Real Bread that slip through the net and become stale. Please think of them not as recipes but as inspiration and swap ingredients in and out according to what you have to hand.

Bread Soup CHRIS YOUNG

With a little research, you'll find many bread soup recipes, from Italian *pappa al pomodoro* and *ribollita*, to Franconian *brotsuppe* and Iceland's unusual *brauðsúpa*. This is a quick and economical member of the family: using homemade chicken stock gets every last bit of value out of the bird, and respects the fact that it died for your dinner. You can use any meat or vegetable stock; at a pinch, a stock/bouillon cube will do, though it won't be as nutritious or as tasty.

SERVES: 2

PREPARATION TIME: 5 minutes

COOKING TIME: 10 minutes

600ml/21fl oz/2½ cups homemade chicken stock (or a mixture of stock and milk)

1 garlic clove, crushed

125g/4½oz/2½ cups chunky breadcrumbs, made from stale white Real Bread

2 eggs (optional)

sea salt and freshly ground black pepper

a drizzle of olive oil, to serve

1. Bring the stock to the boil in a saucepan, add the crushed garlic and simmer for about 5 minutes.

2. Stir in the breadcrumbs and season with salt and pepper. If you are using eggs, break them carefully into the soup at this point. Cover the pan and simmer the soup for a further 4 minutes, which also gives enough time for the eggs to poach.

3. Pour or ladle the soup into two bowls (taking care not to break the eggs, if using) and drizzle a little olive oil into each bowl. Serve immediately.

Liz Wilson took Jane Mason's Virtuous Bread microbakery course in July 2013 and graduated as a Bread Angel. She then spent the following year volunteering in bakeries and cooking schools around London. In April 2014, Liz set up business as Ma Baker, baking loaves for sale and teaching Real Bread skills at her home in Fulham, London. In September that year, Liz won two silver medals at the Tiptree World Bread Awards.

Panzanella LIZ WILSON

This Italian-style salad is a great way of using up any leftover or stale Real Bread, particularly sourdough, which can take up all of the summery flavours and add a chewy texture. As with other recipes in this chapter, there's no one "authentic" version of *panzanella*, and these recipes are more concerned with using up leftovers than with being prescriptive about amounts or ingredients. Just make sure the tomatoes you use are really good sun-ripened ones.

SERVES: 2–4

PREPARATION TIME: 10 minutes
plus 30 minutes standing

1. Tear the bread, crusts on, into pieces the size of unshelled walnuts, then pile them up in a large serving bowl.

2. Add all of the other ingredients and mix together thoroughly – your hands are great tools for this job. Season with salt and pepper.

3. Leave the salad to stand for at least 30 minutes before serving, so the chunks of Real Bread can soak up all of the juices and flavours. If it looks a bit dry, you can add more tomatoes or olive oil.

4–6 thick slices of stale sourdough
Real Bread

80ml/2½fl oz/⅓ cup extra virgin olive
oil, plus extra if needed

2 tbsp red wine vinegar

1 cucumber, diced

1 red onion, finely sliced

6 ripe vine tomatoes, peeled and
roughly chopped, plus extra
if needed

3 garlic cloves, finely chopped

1 handful of torn basil leaves

sea salt and freshly ground black
pepper

Sippet: Depending who you believe, the name might come from a Tuscan dialect word for "little swamp" or standard Italian for bread (*pane*) and little basket (*zanella*).

Breadcrumb Pakoras with Indian Green Chutney CHRIS YOUNG

MAKES: 6 pakoras
PREPARATION TIME: 15 minutes
COOKING TIME: 5 minutes per batch

This recipe conjures up a happy memory of India, of eating freshly fried pakoras from a cone of newspaper in the holy city of Varanasi. It uses breadcrumbs, rather than the usual batter made with gram (chickpea) flour and for me, it is the perfect snack.

FOR THE PAKORAS:

2 large handfuls of freshly made
   breadcumbs, made from Real Bread
1 egg, beaten
1 tbsp plain/all-purpose flour
½ onion, finely diced
1 small handful of coriander/cilantro
   (leaves and stalks), chopped
some curry leaves (enough for a few
   per pakora)
1 small green chilli, chopped (optional)
1 tsp baking powder
½ tsp cumin seeds
½ tsp mustard seeds
½ tsp turmeric
a large pinch of salt
a good grind of black pepper
vegetable oil, for deep-frying

FOR THE GREEN CHUTNEY:

1 large handful of coriander/cilantro
100g/3½oz fresh coconut, grated (or
   desiccated/dried shredded coconut,
   soaked in water until tender and
   drained)
1cm/½in piece of fresh root ginger
1 small green chilli
a few curry leaves
½ tsp mustard seeds
a squeeze of lemon juice
a pinch of salt
sugar, to taste (optional)

1. To make the chutney, blitz together the coriander/cilantro, coconut, ginger and chilli in a food processor to a smoothish paste. Dry-fry the curry leaves and mustard seeds in a frying pan for a couple of minutes to bring out the flavour, and stir these into the chutney, along with the lemon juice, salt and sugar to taste. If the chutney is a little too firm, add a splash of water to make it the desired consistency. Leave to one side while you make the pakoras.

2. Mix all of the pakora ingredients together until combined and you can form the mixture into balls. If the mixture is too dry and you can't shape it, add water little by little until you can; if it seems too wet, add a little more flour.

3. Heat the vegetable oil in a deep, solidly-made pan to 180–190°C/ 350–375°F.

4. Form the mixture into balls about the size of a small chicken's egg and carefully lower a few of them into the hot oil without overcrowding the pan. Fry for about 5 minutes until golden brown, moving them around to ensure they are cooked evenly. Remove with a slotted heatproof spoon and drain on paper towels while you fry the remaining pakoras. Serve with the green chutney on the side.

Baker's Tip: This pakora recipe is a guide, rather than a scientific formula to be adhered to exactly – use whatever spices you like, and other ingredients you might have to hand. For example, you could throw in some small cubes of paneer or strips of chicken, or cooked spinach.

Bread Sauce CHRIS YOUNG

Aromatic and with a discernible, yet silky, texture, this is a traditional British sauce delicious enough to be served with any roast poultry. As this is "leftover cookery", not a science lesson, there's no need to measure the bread exactly (you can even blitz it in a food processor, if you prefer), or to lose sleep over the exact weight of the onion. If you don't have any star anise or one of the other spices, leave it out.

SERVES: 6–8

PREPARATION TIME: 10 minutes, plus 2 hours infusing

COOKING TIME: 15 minutes

600ml/21fl oz/2½ cups milk

1 onion, chopped

2 cloves

1 point from a star anise

1 bay leaf

1 blade of mace

6 black peppercorns, cracked in half

120–150g/4–5½oz/2–2½ cups when prepared white Real Bread, crusts removed and torn or cut into small cubes

1½ tbsp butter

2 tbsp double/heavy cream (optional)

sea salt

1. Put the milk, onion and spices into a saucepan, bring almost to the boil and then remove from the heat. Cover the pan and leave the spices to infuse for at least 2 hours as it cools. You can do this the day before and keep in the refrigerator overnight, if you prefer.

2. Strain the milk, discarding the spices (but keep, or even freeze, the onion to use in another dish at some point).

3. Pour the infused milk back into the pan over a very low heat, add the bread and simmer until the milk has been absorbed and the bread is breaking down.

4. Just before serving, stir in the butter and cream, if using. Taste and if you think it needs a little salt, add a pinch at a time until it is as you prefer.

Baker's Tip: If you have any of this leftover dish left over, I reckon it's good spread on toast . . . carbs on carbs.

Savoury Bread and Butter Pudding KATE DE SYLLAS

If it encourages you to make it, think of this as a cheat's soufflé. I first tried it at a workshop Kate helped our charity's Ethical Eats team to run, and she suggests using fresh seasonal produce for the filling – for example, leeks with wholegrain mustard or slow-roast tomatoes with basil – or making it with leftover cooked meats.

SERVES: 6
PREPARATION TIME: 20 minutes
  plus 20 minutes standing
COOKING TIME: 35 minutes

1. Bring the milk, cream and garlic to a simmer in a saucepan. Remove from the heat and leave to infuse for 20 minutes or until just warm.

2. Meanwhile, grease a large, fairly deep ovenproof dish. Butter the bread slices and arrange half of them in the bottom of the dish. Lay the bacon and asparagus (or your choice of other produce in season) over the bread and scatter with about half of the cheese. Lay the rest of the buttered bread slices on top.

3. Whisk the eggs with the warm milk mixture, a pinch of salt and a few twists of black pepper. Pour this over the bread and scatter the rest of the cheese on top. Leave to stand for about 20 minutes for the bread to soak up some of the milk while you heat the oven to 150°C/130°C fan/300°F/gas 2.

4. Bake the pudding for about 35 minutes, or until the egg mixture is set and the pudding has taken on a golden colour. Serve either still warm or cold.

200ml/7fl oz/¾ cup milk

200ml/7fl oz/¾ cup cream (single/ light or double/heavy will do)

1 or 2 garlic cloves, whole or sliced

75g/2½oz/5 tbsp butter, softened, plus extra for greasing

1 large loaf of any savoury Real Bread, medium sliced

100g/3½oz smoked streaky/side bacon or pancetta, chopped into lardons/small pieces

10–15 asparagus spears, when in season locally

200g/7oz/2½ cups grated Gruyère or other hard cheese

100g/3½oz/1¼ cups grated Parmesan cheese

3 eggs

sea salt and freshly ground black pepper

Kate de Syllas spent two decades cooking, growing, talking and sometimes even working in kitchens, gardens, charities and social enterprises in east London. She is now the owner-chef at Hantverk & Found in Margate, Kent. She cooks sustainable seafood and loves leftovers and Real Bread.

Mushroom, Red Pepper and Paneer Loaf CHRIS YOUNG

You can adapt this recipe to use ingredients you like, or have to hand. No tarragon? Use basil or chives. No paneer? Use halloumi (and reduce the salt). If you've got some bacon that needs using up, stir it in, or add a handful of seeds or chopped nuts for more texture.

SERVES: 4–6

PREPARATION TIME: 20 minutes

COOKING TIME: 1¼ hours

1. Heat 2 tablespoons of the oil in a frying pan and fry the onions until translucent, stirring occasionally. Add the peppers and fry for a few minutes more until softened.

2. Meanwhile, put the breadcrumbs in a large mixing bowl with the paneer. Add the cooked onions and peppers to the breadcrumbs.

3. Heat the remaining oil and cook the mushrooms over a medium heat with the lid on, stirring occasionally, until they release their juice. Leave them to simmer for a few minutes and then strain off the juice and reserve. Add half of the mushrooms to the breadcrumb mixture, leaving the remainder to cool slightly.

4. Put the eggs, two-thirds of the cream cheese, the tomato purée/paste, salt and a few generous grinds of pepper with the cooled mushrooms in a food processor and pulse until it forms a coarse paste. Add this and the tarragon to the breadcrumbs and stir until thoroughly mixed.

5. Heat the oven to 180°C/160°C fan/350°F/gas 4. Grease a 1kg/2lb loaf tin well, scrape the mixture into it and smooth the top with a spatula. Bake for 30 minutes, then turn the tin round and bake for another 30–35 minutes.

6. Meanwhile, make a sauce by heating the reserved mushroom juice in a pan, whisking in the remaining cream cheese and adding salt and pepper to taste. Serve the loaf with the mushroom sauce on the side.

3 tbsp vegetable oil or butter, plus extra for greasing

2 onions, sliced

2 red peppers, sliced

150g/5½oz/2½ cups coarse breadcrumbs, made from stale Real Bread

200g/7oz paneer cheese

500g/1lb 2oz mushrooms, diced or sliced

3 eggs

150g/5½oz/⅔ cup full-fat cream cheese

3 tbsp tomato purée/paste

1 tsp salt

freshly ground black pepper

a sprig or two of fresh tarragon, chopped

Sourdough Pancakes CHRIS YOUNG

MAKES: about 8 pancakes

PREPARATION TIME: overnight plus 5 minutes

COOKING TIME: 3–4 minutes per batch

Sometimes you'll find yourself with more sourdough starter than you can use. Rather than just throw it away, ask if anyone you know might like some, with a baking session to get them into making sourdough loaves for themselves. Or think about what else you can make with it – starting with these pancakes.

100g/3½oz/scant 1 cup white sourdough starter

30–50g/1–1¾oz/3½–6 tbsp plain/all-purpose flour

3½ tbsp milk

1 egg

1 tsp caster/superfine sugar

½–¾ tsp bicarbonate of soda/baking soda

butter, for frying, plus more butter or syrup to serve

NB: A bread dough made with chemical leavening would fall outside the Campaign's definition of Real Bread, but we have no view on using bicarbonate of soda/baking soda for other purposes: say, as a dipping solution for pretzels, or in other foods such as cakes or pancakes.

1. Whisk the sourdough starter with most of the flour. Cover and leave at room temperature overnight.

2. The next day, whisk in the remaining flour and other pancake ingredients to make a stiff batter.

3. Melt a small amount of butter in a frying pan, over a medium-high heat. Pour in spoonfuls of batter to form circles about 10–15cm/4–6in in diameter. Cook for a few minutes until set on top and lightly browned underneath.

4. Use a spatula or fish slice to turn the pancakes over and cook for a few minutes more until lightly browned on the other side. Remove from the pan and keep warm while you make more pancakes with the remaining batter. Serve with melted butter, your favourite syrup, or other choice of topping.

Baker's Tip: You can also make French crêpe-style pancakes from leftover starter. Simply whisk together 400g/14oz/1¾ cups sourdough starter of any type, 1 egg and ¾ tsp fine/table salt. Melt a small amount of butter in a frying pan over a medium-high heat. Pour in just enough batter to coat the bottom of the pan thinly and swirl it around. Cook for a few minutes until set and lightly browned underneath. Using a spatula or fish slice, flip the pancake over and cook for a few minutes more on the other side. Serve at once with your favourite topping, or reserve under a clean cloth while you make more pancakes from the rest of the batter in the same way.

Masala Chai-Spiced Bread and Butter Pudding CHRIS YOUNG

I started making bread and butter pudding when I was in my teens. Because I couldn't leave a recipe alone, I would throw in different ingredients each time. This version came after backpacking around India in the late 1990s, drinking endless glasses of *masala chai* (chai tea latte), their spiced and usually very sweet take on tea.

SERVES: 4–6

PREPARATION TIME: 20 minutes plus 30 minutes soaking

COOKING TIME: 45 minutes

1. Start by making the custard. Pour the milk into a saucepan, add the spices, vanilla and a twist or two of pepper, and heat but do not boil. Remove from the heat, cover and leave to cool and infuse.

2. Grease an ovenproof dish. Butter the bread on one side and arrange half of the slices in a layer in the dish. Scatter the lemon zest and raisins over the bread and layer the rest of the bread on top with the points of the triangles sticking up.

3. Strain the spices out of the infused milk. Split the vanilla pod/bean lengthways and scrape the seeds back into the milk (dry the vanilla pod/bean to use again, or to flavour a jar of sugar).

4. Whisk together the sugar and eggs, then add the milk and whisk again. Pour the custard over the bread and fruit in the dish – it should reach about halfway up the top layer of bread. Press the bread down into the mixture and leave to soak for about 30 minutes. Meanwhile, heat the oven to 180°C/160°C fan/350°F/gas 4.

5. Melt a little butter and use a pastry brush to brush it over any bread that may be peeking out above the custard mixture. Bake the pudding for 30–40 minutes until brown on top and just set in the middle – it should be wobbly, not watery. Serve warm or cold with cream or custard.

300g/10½oz stale Real Bread, sliced into triangles about 1cm/½in thick

50g/1¾oz/3½ tbsp butter, plus extra for greasing and brushing

zest of ½ lemon

50g/1¾oz/⅓ cup seedless raisins or sultanas/golden raisins

FOR THE CUSTARD:

600ml/21fl oz/2½ cups milk (or a mixture of milk and cream)

1 green cardamom pod

1 or 2 cloves

1 slice (about 3mm/⅛in thick) fresh root ginger

2cm/¾in piece of cinnamon quill or cassia bark

1 vanilla pod/bean

freshly ground black pepper

50g/1¾oz/¼ cup caster/superfine sugar

2 eggs

Baker's Tip: This can be made with whatever plain or sweet Real Bread needs using up. All of the measurements are approximate; you can adjust the amounts of bread, butter or sugar according to taste.

Gingery Treacle Tart KATE DE SYLLAS

Used as a lure by The Childcatcher in *Chitty Chitty Bang Bang*, this classic British pudding is all sorts of wrong. The main ingredient is a by-product of industrial sugar refining. On the misleading marketing front, it doesn't however contain any treacle: just traditional golden syrup, a British favourite since the 19th century. You could replace half of the syrup with honey, not that it'd make it any healthier.

MAKES: 1 large (28cm/11in) tart
PREPARATION TIME: 15 minutes
BAKING TIME: 45 minutes

FOR THE PASTRY:
225g/8oz/1¾ cups plain/all-purpose flour
110g/3¾oz/½ cup butter (salted or unsalted) chilled and cut into cubes, plus extra for greasing
1 egg, beaten

FOR THE FILLING:
450g/1lb/1⅓ cups golden syrup/light corn syrup
85g/3oz/1½ cups freshly made Real Bread crumbs, coarse rather than fine
1 tsp ground ginger, or grated fresh root ginger, or to taste
zest of ½ lemon and about 2 tsp of its juice
zest of ½ orange and about 4 tsp of its juice

cream or custard, to serve

1. Heat the oven to 190°C/170°C fan/375°F/gas 5 and grease a loose-bottomed 28cm/11in tart tin.

2. In a large bowl, rub the flour and butter together with your fingertips until it has the texture of breadcrumbs.

3. Mix the egg in with a knife, and then work the pastry until it just comes together – don't overwork it, or it'll become tough and plasticky.

4. Flour the work surface and a rolling pin, and roll the pastry out into a circle large enough to fit the bottom and sides of the tart tin. Leave the pastry to rest for 5–10 minutes to reduce the risk of it shrinking back.

5. Line the tart tin with the pastry and prick it all over with a fork. Scatter with ceramic baking beans/pie weights (or dried peas or macaroni) to prevent large blisters bubbling up. Bake for about 12 minutes until cooked but still pale. Remove the baking beans/pie weights and continue to bake for another 2–3 minutes until the base is lightly golden.

6. Meanwhile, mix all of the filling ingredients together. Take the case out of the oven and spoon in the filling, pressing it down slightly to make sure it is evenly distributed and to avoid air bubbles. Level the top with a spatula and bake for a further 30 minutes.

7. Leave to cool on a wire rack until just slightly warm, and serve with cream or custard.

Beyond Your Kitchen

So, you've got the hang of this Real Bread making thing, friends and family are telling you "you could sell that, darl", but where can you go from here? Well, why not start a microbakery from home, or get together with people round your way to set up a Community Supported Bakery?

Microbakery

This is perhaps the most exciting and vibrant area of the Real Bread movement. In my job at the Real Bread Campaign, it feels like I hear from people every month who have become so sick at being unable to find anything but industrial loaves in their neck of the woods, that they've said "sod it – *I'll be my local baker*", or words to that effect. If you have an oven, you can be your local community's baker, even if you just bake half a dozen loaves to order, once a week, for people on your street, or 30 loaves to sell at a local farmers' market. Ask your local authority what food safety, hygiene and other regulations you need to meet, to set up your own microbusiness.

Community Supported Baking

There is no hard and fast definition of a Community Supported Bakery (CSB). What sets a CSB apart from other bakeries, some of which might see themselves as community bakeries, is that its business model blurs the traditional "me baker/you customer" set up, in which the baker lays out his or her wares, hopes that people will come along to buy

them, and then keeps any profit made. In the case of a CSB, people from the local community join the baker as what the Slow Food movement calls "co-producers" by making some sort of longer-term investment in the business and so sharing at least some of the risks and rewards.

CSB models

Here are just some ways people can join together as a community to run a Real Bread bakery.

* Community ownership: The CSB could be run as a worker-owned cooperative or owned by local people buying into a community share or loan scheme.

* Bread as bread: One form of CSB support is a "bread bonds" scheme that offers investors their dividends, interest payments or even capital repayment in bread.

* In-kind investments: CSBers can waive/reduce their charges for property rental, flour, grain, milling, equipment, labour for fitting out the bakery, shifts running the shop, shifts in the bakehouse, adding the bakery's bread to their own delivery rounds, or helping with accounts, ordering or marketing.

NB: To be a true CSB, supporters should pay more than just lip service to one or more of these types of investment. For example, a bakery where subscription payments account for only a few percent of turnover isn't a CSB.

Bookshelf

I've got several bookshelves filled with doughy tomes, not all of which I can include here, so these are some I referred to while researching and writing this book.

Manna, Walter Banfield, McLaren (1937)

English Bread and Yeast Cookery, Elizabeth David, Allen Lane (1977)

Artisan Baking, Maggie Glezer, Workman Publishing (2000)

Bread: A Baker's Book of Techniques and Recipes, Jeffrey Hamelman, John Wiley & Sons (2004)

Breadcraft, J.R. Irons, Virtue and Company, (1948)

Six Thousand Years of Bread: Its Holy and Unholy History, H.E. Jacob, The Lyons Press (1997)

The Modern Baker, Confectioner and Caterer, John Kirkland, Gresham Books (1907)

Bread: A Slice of History, John Marchant, Bryan Reuben and Joan Alcock, The History Press (2008)

Traditional Food of Britain, Laura Mason and Catherine Brown, Prospect Books (2004)

McGee on Food & Cooking, Harold McGee, Hodder and Stoughton (2004)

Bread Matters, Andrew Whitley, Fourth Estate (2006)

Sustain publications

Every year Sustain produces a wide range of reports, guides and magazines on healthy and ethical food. They include:

Knead to Know: The Real Bread Starter
The Campaign's introductory guide to becoming enterprising with a microbakery or CSB. (Sustain, 2011/Grub Street, 2013)

Rising Up The Real Bread Campaign report on the therapeutic and social benefits that Real Bread making offers to people living with mental health issues, or otherwise facing a tougher time than most of us. (2013)

Bake Your Lawn Follow the Real Bread journey from seed to sandwich with our guide on how to take a handful of wheat and grow it, mill it, bake it, eat it. (2011)

Are Supermarket Bloomers Pants? The Real Bread Campaign's investigation into what really lies behind supermarket in-store "bakery" loaves. (2010)

Lessons in Loaf A teachers' guide to bringing Real Bread making into the classroom, with suggestions for using bread as a topic across a wide range of curriculum subjects. (2009)

True Loaf The quarterly magazine exclusively for Real Bread Campaign supporters. (2009- present)

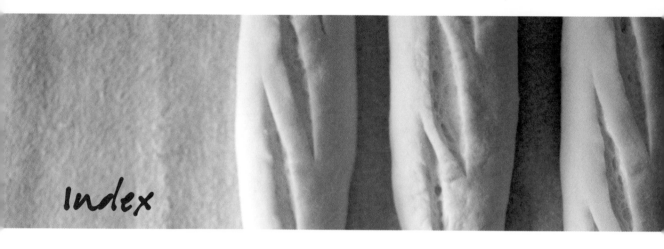

Index